Name:

Address:

COVER PHOTOGRAPH

THE GAZE
Barb Snyder

During a photography course in Florence, I happily drank in the abundance of art. Wandering the Pitti Palace I noticed a classmate who could surely have been a subject of Titian's, gazing raptly at his painting of Mary Magdalene. In the next room was a classical statue of a woman gazing over her shoulder. The gazes multiply into a dialogue: "who is gazing at who?"

Women throughout history have been cast by the male painter's gaze as muse, as soulmate, as subject, as erotic object. Ambiguities abound, a source for reflection and critique for women through the centuries.

THE WOMEN'S DAYBOOK

2·0·1·0

Imagining Women

Creativity & the Arts

SUMACH PRESS

LUNAR CYCLE:

New Moon ●
First Quarter ☽
Full Moon ○
Last Quarter ☾

Copyright © 2009 Sumach Press

Printed and bound in Canada

ISBN 978-1-894549-81-3

SUMACH PRESS

An Imprint of Canadian Scholars' Press Inc.

180 Bloor Street West, Suite 801
Toronto, Ontario
M5S 2V6

info@sumachpress.com
www.sumachpress.com

Preface

Gazes echo throughout our cover photograph this year — male gazes embodied in centuries-old paintings and sculptures that encode the legacy of patriarchal naming, the questioning female gaze that confronts them. Female artists have always played a key role in imagining lives beyond the Madonna/Eve/Crone constellation, beyond constructs which have objectified and constrained us for so long. Our photographers this year explore women's telling of their own stories, their own sense of agency, through art. As October's photographer Jill Glessing says, old wives' tales and village whispers have swelled to stake an equal claim in the world of words. Out of female experience has emerged an insistence on the legitimacy of personal and domestic subjects, side by side with an unyielding commentary on social and political spaces. Searching for balance between work, children, relationships and wider society, women artists have documented and creatively transformed our understandings of ways society can work. Quiet meditations; moments of play, of satire, of outrage; images that peel back surfaces to reveal the fragilities, strengths, the poetry rippling beneath — these are threads gathered up by this year's photographers as they stitch women into the fabric of society, imagining women through the lens of the arts.

JANUARY

▽

LOUISE LECAVALIER/
LA LA LA HUMAN STEPS

Linda Dawn Hammond

In 1985, Montreal choreographer Édouard Lock invited me to photograph a live performance of his dance troupe, "La La La Human Steps." The piece, entitled "Human Sex," employed rock music and multimedia and featured Lock's incomparable muse and principal dancer, Louise Lecavalier.

As she hurtled through the air, a whirl of bleached blonde dreadlocks, it was startling to witness the muscular intensity of a female body pushed beyond all boundaries of gender. Dancing with a controlled recklessness, Lecavalier created a new language of gestures, at once intimate and aggressive, with which to challenge and redefine human relationships. All this, combined with the face of an angel upon whose upper lip a moustache had been crudely drawn, intended to disturb any complacent reverie on her apparent beauty.

As a photographer, I subscribe to Cartier-Bresson's philosophy of the "decisive moment," which can be applied to all documentary subjects, including dance and music. If successful, the resultant image transcends a merely descriptive function to embody a more universal truth. In dance photography, one relies on skill, but more importantly, on intuition, to anticipate the arc of a gesture and be prepared to seize it before it has even manifested itself.

MONTH-AT-A-GLANCE PLANNER

JANUARY

Sunday	Monday	Tuesday	Wednesday	Thursday	Friday	Saturday
					1	2
3	4	5	6	☾ 7	8	9
10	11	12	13	14	● 15	16
17	18	19	20	21	22	☽ 23
24 / 31	25	26	27	28	29	○ 30

JANUARY 2010

PROJECTS	*1* FRIDAY	*2* SATURDAY
	New Year's Day	

3 SUNDAY

TO DO LIST

NOTES

JANUARY

JANUARY						
S	M	T	W	T	F	S
					1	2
3	4	5	6	7	8	9
10	11	12	13	14	15	16
17	18	19	20	21	22	23
24	25	26	27	28	29	30
31						

4 MONDAY | 5 TUESDAY | 6 WEDNESDAY

Birth of Guru Gobind Singh Sahib — *Epiphany*

4 MONDAY	5 TUESDAY	6 WEDNESDAY
8:00	8:00	8:00
9:00	9:00	9:00
10:00	10:00	10:00
11:00	11:00	11:00
12:00	12:00	12:00
1:00	1:00	1:00
2:00	2:00	2:00
3:00	3:00	3:00
4:00	4:00	4:00
5:00	5:00	5:00
6:00	6:00	6:00
Evening	Evening	Evening
To Do	To Do	To Do

FEBRUARY
S M T W T F S
     1 2 3 4 5 6
7 8 9 10 11 12 13
14 15 16 17 18 19 20
21 22 23 24 25 26 27
28

2010

7 THURSDAY ☾	8 FRIDAY	9 SATURDAY
Orthodox Christmas		
8:00	8:00	
9:00	9:00	
10:00	10:00	
11:00	11:00	
12:00	12:00	**10** SUNDAY
1:00	1:00	
2:00	2:00	
3:00	3:00	
4:00	4:00	
5:00	5:00	
6:00	6:00	N O T E S
EVENING	EVENING	
TO DO	TO DO	

JANUARY

JANUARY
S M T W T F S
              1 2
3 4 5 6 7 8 9
10 11 12 13 14 15 16
17 18 19 20 21 22 23
24 25 26 27 28 29 30
31

11 MONDAY	**12** TUESDAY	**13** WEDNESDAY
8:00	8:00	8:00
9:00	9:00	9:00
10:00	10:00	10:00
11:00	11:00	11:00
12:00	12:00	12:00
1:00	1:00	1:00
2:00	2:00	2:00
3:00	3:00	3:00
4:00	4:00	4:00
5:00	5:00	5:00
6:00	6:00	6:00
Evening	Evening	Evening
To Do	To Do	To Do

FEBRUARY
S M T W T F S
       1 2 3 4 5 6
7 8 9 10 11 12 13
14 15 16 17 18 19 20
21 22 23 24 25 26 27
28

2010

14 THURSDAY	15 FRIDAY ●	16 SATURDAY
	Annular Solar Eclipse	
8:00	8:00	
9:00	9:00	
10:00	10:00	
11:00	11:00	
12:00	12:00	17 SUNDAY
1:00	1:00	
2:00	2:00	
3:00	3:00	
4:00	4:00	
5:00	5:00	
6:00	6:00	N O T E S
EVENING	EVENING	
To Do	To Do	

JANUARY

JANUARY
S M T W T F S
          1 2
3 4 5 6 7 8 9
10 11 12 13 14 15 16
17 18 19 20 21 22 23
24 25 26 27 28 29 30
31

18 MONDAY	19 TUESDAY	20 WEDNESDAY
Martin Luther King Jr. Day		*Vasant Panchami*
8:00	8:00	8:00
9:00	9:00	9:00
10:00	10:00	10:00
11:00	11:00	11:00
12:00	12:00	12:00
1:00	1:00	1:00
2:00	2:00	2:00
3:00	3:00	3:00
4:00	4:00	4:00
5:00	5:00	5:00
6:00	6:00	6:00
EVENING	EVENING	EVENING
To Do	To Do	To Do

FEBRUARY

S	M	T	W	T	F	S
	1	2	3	4	5	6
7	8	9	10	11	12	13
14	15	16	17	18	19	20
21	22	23	24	25	26	27
28						

2010

21 THURSDAY | **22** FRIDAY | **23** SATURDAY

8:00
9:00
10:00
11:00
12:00

24 SUNDAY

1:00
2:00
3:00
4:00
5:00
6:00

NOTES

Evening

To Do

JANUARY

JANUARY
S M T W T F S
1 2
3 4 5 6 7 8 9
10 11 12 13 14 15 16
17 18 19 20 21 22 23
24 25 26 27 28 29 30
31

25 MONDAY | 26 TUESDAY | 27 WEDNESDAY

International Holocaust Memorial Day

MONDAY	TUESDAY	WEDNESDAY
8:00	8:00	8:00
9:00	9:00	9:00
10:00	10:00	10:00
11:00	11:00	11:00
12:00	12:00	12:00
1:00	1:00	1:00
2:00	2:00	2:00
3:00	3:00	3:00
4:00	4:00	4:00
5:00	5:00	5:00
6:00	6:00	6:00
Evening	Evening	Evening
To Do	To Do	To Do

FEBRUARY

S	M	T	W	T	F	S
	1	2	3	4	5	6
7	8	9	10	11	12	13
14	15	16	17	18	19	20
21	22	23	24	25	26	27
28						

2010

28 THURSDAY	29 FRIDAY	30 SATURDAY ○
		Mahayana New Year
		Tu B'Shvat
8:00	8:00	
9:00	9:00	
10:00	10:00	
11:00	11:00	
12:00	12:00	**31 SUNDAY**
1:00	1:00	
2:00	2:00	
3:00	3:00	
4:00	4:00	
5:00	5:00	
6:00	6:00	N O T E S
Evening	Evening	
To Do	To Do	

FEBRUARY

▽

CREATIVE ENDEAVOURS

Judith Lermer Crawley

Montreal painter Marion Wagschal, a close friend since our student days in the 1960s, is caught in a shaft of light during my visit to her studio. She stands close to her painting *Burning Spoons* (1994), in which she sits bolt upright in bed as her mother naps.

Marion remarks about the work: "It's all about memory—many of the memories of our family have gone up in flames."

I feel privileged to have captured a moment that crosses generations and recalls the absence in my own life of family members and mementos from pre-Holocaust Europe.

MONTH-AT-A-GLANCE PLANNER

FEBRUARY

Sunday	Monday	Tuesday	Wednesday	Thursday	Friday	Saturday
	1	2	3	4	☾ 5	6
7	8	9	10	11	12	● 13
14	15	16	17	18	19	20
☽ 21	22	23	24	25	26	27
○ 28						

FEBRUARY *2010*

ONGOING PROJECTS DUE BY

TO DO LIST

FEBRUARY

FEBRUARY
S M T W T F S
1 2 3 4 5 6
7 8 9 10 11 12 13
14 15 16 17 18 19 20
21 22 23 24 25 26 27
28

1 MONDAY	*2* TUESDAY	*3* WEDNESDAY
Black History Month	*Groundhog Day*	*Setsubun*
8:00	8:00	8:00
9:00	9:00	9:00
10:00	10:00	10:00
11:00	11:00	11:00
12:00	12:00	12:00
1:00	1:00	1:00
2:00	2:00	2:00
3:00	3:00	3:00
4:00	4:00	4:00
5:00	5:00	5:00
6:00	6:00	6:00
Evening	Evening	Evening
To Do	To Do	To Do

MARCH						
S	M	T	W	T	F	S
	1	2	3	4	5	6
7	8	9	10	11	12	13
14	15	16	17	18	19	20
21	22	23	24	25	26	27
28	29	30	31			

2010

4 THURSDAY	5 FRIDAY ☾	6 SATURDAY
8:00	8:00	
9:00	9:00	
10:00	10:00	
11:00	11:00	
12:00	12:00	**7 SUNDAY**
1:00	1:00	
2:00	2:00	
3:00	3:00	
4:00	4:00	
5:00	5:00	
6:00	6:00	NOTES
Evening	Evening	
To Do	To Do	

FEBRUARY

FEBRUARY
S M T W T F S
1 2 3 4 5 6
7 8 9 10 11 12 13
14 15 16 17 18 19 20
21 22 23 24 25 26 27
28

8 MONDAY	*9* TUESDAY	*10* WEDNESDAY
8:00	8:00	8:00
9:00	9:00	9:00
10:00	10:00	10:00
11:00	11:00	11:00
12:00	12:00	12:00
1:00	1:00	1:00
2:00	2:00	2:00
3:00	3:00	3:00
4:00	4:00	4:00
5:00	5:00	5:00
6:00	6:00	6:00
EVENING	EVENING	EVENING
To Do	To Do	To Do

MARCH
S M T W T F S
1 2 3 4 5 6
7 8 9 10 11 12 13
14 15 16 17 18 19 20
21 22 23 24 25 26 27
28 29 30 31

2010

11 THURSDAY	**12** FRIDAY	**13** SATURDAY ●
	Maha Shivaratri	
8:00	8:00	
9:00	9:00	
10:00	10:00	
11:00	11:00	
12:00	12:00	**14** SUNDAY
1:00	1:00	*Valentine's Day*
		Lunar New Year
2:00	2:00	
3:00	3:00	
4:00	4:00	
5:00	5:00	
6:00	6:00	N O T E S
EVENING	EVENING	
TO DO	TO DO	

FEBRUARY

FEBRUARY
S M T W T F S
　　　1　2　3　4　5　6
7　8　9　10　11　12　13
14　15　16　17　18　19　20
21　22　23　24　25　26　27
28

15 MONDAY	*16* TUESDAY	*17* WEDNESDAY
Provincial Holiday (ON, AB, SK, MB)	*Shrove Tuesday*	*Ash Wednesday / Lent Begins*
8:00	8:00	8:00
9:00	9:00	9:00
10:00	10:00	10:00
11:00	11:00	11:00
12:00	12:00	12:00
1:00	1:00	1:00
2:00	2:00	2:00
3:00	3:00	3:00
4:00	4:00	4:00
5:00	5:00	5:00
6:00	6:00	6:00
Evening	Evening	Evening
To Do	To Do	To Do

MARCH						
S	M	T	W	T	F	S
	1	2	3	4	5	6
7	8	9	10	11	12	13
14	15	16	17	18	19	20
21	22	23	24	25	26	27
28	29	30	31			

2010

18 THURSDAY	19 FRIDAY	20 SATURDAY
8:00	8:00	
9:00	9:00	
10:00	10:00	
11:00	11:00	
12:00	12:00	**21 SUNDAY**
1:00	1:00	
2:00	2:00	
3:00	3:00	
4:00	4:00	
5:00	5:00	
6:00	6:00	NOTES
EVENING	EVENING	
To Do	To Do	

FEBRUARY

FEBRUARY
S M T W T F S
1 2 3 4 5 6
7 8 9 10 11 12 13
14 15 16 17 18 19 20
21 22 23 24 25 26 27
28

22 MONDAY	23 TUESDAY	24 WEDNESDAY
8:00	8:00	8:00
9:00	9:00	9:00
10:00	10:00	10:00
11:00	11:00	11:00
12:00	12:00	12:00
1:00	1:00	1:00
2:00	2:00	2:00
3:00	3:00	3:00
4:00	4:00	4:00
5:00	5:00	5:00
6:00	6:00	6:00
Evening	Evening	Evening
To Do	To Do	To Do

MARCH

S	M	T	W	T	F	S
	1	2	3	4	5	6
7	8	9	10	11	12	13
14	15	16	17	18	19	20
21	22	23	24	25	26	27
28	29	30	31			

2010

---

25 THURSDAY | **26 FRIDAY** | **27 SATURDAY**

Eve of Purim

8:00	8:00
9:00	9:00
10:00	10:00
11:00	11:00
12:00	12:00

28 SUNDAY

Holi begins

1:00	1:00
2:00	2:00
3:00	3:00
4:00	4:00
5:00	5:00
6:00	6:00

NOTES

EVENING | EVENING

To Do | To Do

MARCH

▽

THE CLICHETTES
From FACES OF FEMINISM/*Toronto*

PAMELA HARRIS

The women's movement came by its anger legitimately—there's been lots to be angry about. But it has also encompassed much irreverent play. The Clichettes took the mickey on male and popular culture—inflating it till it exploded in our faces. In the doorway to this men's clothing store, we get a double vision of dressing up as they mock the swagger and style promoted on the other side of the glass.

Photography, like acting, is transformation—The Clichettes turn themselves into men; my camera turns their moving, colourful world into one that is still, and black and white. Both are illusions, and we humans delight in illusion as we do in laughter.

Long may we laugh, long may we play, long may we deflate the powerful and overblown. Humour, like the arts, is fuel and ballast.

MONTH-AT-A-GLANCE PLANNER

			MARCH			
SUNDAY	MONDAY	TUESDAY	WEDNESDAY	THURSDAY	FRIDAY	SATURDAY
	1	*2*	*3*	*4*	*5*	*6*
☾ *7*	*8*	*9*	*10*	*11*	*12*	*13*
14	● *15*	*16*	*17*	*18*	*19*	*20*
21	*22*	☽ *23*	*24*	*25*	*26*	*27*
28	○ *29*	*30*	*31*			

MARCH 2010

ONGOING PROJECTS · DUE BY

TO DO LIST

MARCH

MARCH
S M T W T F S
       1 2 3 4 5 6
 7 8 9 10 11 12 13
14 15 16 17 18 19 20
21 22 23 24 25 26 27
28 29 30 31

1 MONDAY	*2* TUESDAY	*3* WEDNESDAY
Hola Mohala		
8:00	8:00	8:00
9:00	9:00	9:00
10:00	10:00	10:00
11:00	11:00	11:00
12:00	12:00	12:00
1:00	1:00	1:00
2:00	2:00	2:00
3:00	3:00	3:00
4:00	4:00	4:00
5:00	5:00	5:00
6:00	6:00	6:00
EVENING	EVENING	EVENING
TO DO	TO DO	TO DO

APRIL

S	M	T	W	T	F	S
				1	2	3
4	5	6	7	8	9	10
11	12	13	14	15	16	17
18	19	20	21	22	23	24
25	26	27	28	29	30	

2010

4 THURSDAY	5 FRIDAY	6 SATURDAY
	Women's World Day of Prayer	
8:00	8:00	
9:00	9:00	
10:00	10:00	
11:00	11:00	
12:00	12:00	**7 SUNDAY** ☾
1:00	1:00	
2:00	2:00	
3:00	3:00	
4:00	4:00	
5:00	5:00	
6:00	6:00	**NOTES**
EVENING	EVENING	
To Do	To Do	

MARCH

MARCH
S M T W T F S
         1 2 3 4 5 6
 7 8 9 10 11 12 13
14 15 16 17 18 19 20
21 22 23 24 25 26 27
28 29 30 31

8 MONDAY	9 TUESDAY	10 WEDNESDAY
Commonwealth Day		
International Women's Day		
8:00	8:00	8:00
9:00	9:00	9:00
10:00	10:00	10:00
11:00	11:00	11:00
12:00	12:00	12:00
1:00	1:00	1:00
2:00	2:00	2:00
3:00	3:00	3:00
4:00	4:00	4:00
5:00	5:00	5:00
6:00	6:00	6:00
Evening	Evening	Evening
To Do	To Do	To Do

APRIL
S	M	T	W	T	F	S
				1	2	3
4	5	6	7	8	9	10
11	12	13	14	15	16	17
18	19	20	21	22	23	24
25	26	27	28	29	30	

2010

11 THURSDAY	12 FRIDAY	13 SATURDAY
8:00	8:00	
9:00	9:00	
10:00	10:00	
11:00	11:00	
12:00	12:00	**14 SUNDAY**
1:00	1:00	*Daylight Saving Time begins*
2:00	2:00	
3:00	3:00	
4:00	4:00	
5:00	5:00	
6:00	6:00	NOTES
EVENING	EVENING	
TO DO	TO DO	

MARCH

MARCH
S M T W T F S
1 2 3 4 5 6
7 8 9 10 11 12 13
14 15 16 17 18 19 20
21 22 23 24 25 26 27
28 29 30 31

15 MONDAY ●	*16* TUESDAY	*17* WEDNESDAY
		St. Patrick's Day
8:00	8:00	8:00
9:00	9:00	9:00
10:00	10:00	10:00
11:00	11:00	11:00
12:00	12:00	12:00
1:00	1:00	1:00
2:00	2:00	2:00
3:00	3:00	3:00
4:00	4:00	4:00
5:00	5:00	5:00
6:00	6:00	6:00
EVENING	EVENING	EVENING
To Do	To Do	To Do

APRIL

S	M	T	W	T	F	S
				1	2	3
4	5	6	7	8	9	10
11	12	13	14	15	16	17
18	19	20	21	22	23	24
25	26	27	28	29	30	

2010

18 THURSDAY	*19* FRIDAY	*20* SATURDAY
		Vernal Equinox
8:00	8:00	
9:00	9:00	
10:00	10:00	
11:00	11:00	
12:00	12:00	*21* SUNDAY
1:00	1:00	*Naw-Ruz*
2:00	2:00	
3:00	3:00	
4:00	4:00	
5:00	5:00	
6:00	6:00	NOTES
EVENING	EVENING	
TO DO	TO DO	

MARCH

MARCH
S M T W T F S
1 2 3 4 5 6
7 8 9 10 11 12 13
14 15 16 17 18 19 20
21 22 23 24 25 26 27
28 29 30 31

22 MONDAY	23 TUESDAY ☽	24 WEDNESDAY
8:00	8:00	8:00
9:00	9:00	9:00
10:00	10:00	10:00
11:00	11:00	11:00
12:00	12:00	12:00
1:00	1:00	1:00
2:00	2:00	2:00
3:00	3:00	3:00
4:00	4:00	4:00
5:00	5:00	5:00
6:00	6:00	6:00
Evening	Evening	Evening
To Do	To Do	To Do

APRIL

S	M	T	W	T	F	S
				1	2	3
4	5	6	7	8	9	10
11	12	13	14	15	16	17
18	19	20	21	22	23	24
25	26	27	28	29	30	

2010

25 THURSDAY	26 FRIDAY	27 SATURDAY
		Earth Hour Day *
8:00	8:00	
9:00	9:00	
10:00	10:00	
11:00	11:00	
12:00	12:00	**28 SUNDAY**
		Palm Sunday
1:00	1:00	
2:00	2:00	
3:00	3:00	
4:00	4:00	
5:00	5:00	
6:00	6:00	**NOTES**
Evening	Evening	* *Turn off your lights for sixty minutes on this day for Earth Hour, a global World Wildlife Fund initiative to raise awareness about global warming.*
To Do	To Do	

MARCH

MARCH
S M T W T F S
         1 2 3 4 5 6
 7 8 9 10 11 12 13
14 15 16 17 18 19 20
21 22 23 24 25 26 27
28 29 30 31

29 MONDAY ○	30 TUESDAY	31 WEDNESDAY
Eve of Passover		
8:00	8:00	8:00
9:00	9:00	9:00
10:00	10:00	10:00
11:00	11:00	11:00
12:00	12:00	12:00
1:00	1:00	1:00
2:00	2:00	2:00
3:00	3:00	3:00
4:00	4:00	4:00
5:00	5:00	5:00
6:00	6:00	6:00
EVENING	EVENING	EVENING
To Do	To Do	To Do

APRIL

S	M	T	W	T	F	S
				1	2	3
4	5	6	7	8	9	10
11	12	13	14	15	16	17
18	19	20	21	22	23	24
25	26	27	28	29	30	

2010

NOTES

APRIL

▽

ANNE STEVENS
VIRGINIA MAK

Anne Stevens kicks up her heels.

Anne got it into her head to become an architect as a teenager. Her parents showered her with drafting and drawing tools, and she kept at it until graduation in London, England.

Working as an independent architect can be demanding: always the attention to detail, sometimes the winning over of male colleagues who belong to the "old school." But Anne finds creativity in her work: the initial drawings, putting together presentations, photographing a building at different stages of completion.

Anne also has a passion for designing treehouses. In her view, bringing a sense of fun to adult architecture is important. Buildings should be structures one enjoys making, like a child building a fort. Her company is called Fort Architect.

MONTH-AT-A-GLANCE PLANNER

APRIL						
SUNDAY	MONDAY	TUESDAY	WEDNESDAY	THURSDAY	FRIDAY	SATURDAY
				1	2	3
4	5	☾ 6	7	8	9	10
11	12	13	● 14	15	16	17
18	19	20	☽ 21	22	23	24
25	26	27	○ 28	29	30	

APRIL   2010

1 THURSDAY	2 FRIDAY	3 SATURDAY
April Fool's Day	*Good Friday*	
8:00	8:00	
9:00	9:00	
10:00	10:00	
11:00	11:00	
12:00	12:00	**4 SUNDAY**
1:00	1:00	*Easter Sunday*
		Orthodox Easter
2:00	2:00	
3:00	3:00	
4:00	4:00	
5:00	5:00	
6:00	6:00	N O T E S
EVENING	EVENING	
To Do	To Do	

APRIL

APRIL						
S	M	T	W	T	F	S
			1	2	3
4	5	6	7	8	9	10
11	12	13	14	15	16	17
18	19	20	21	22	23	24
25	26	27	28	29	30	

5 MONDAY	6 TUESDAY ☾	7 WEDNESDAY
Easter Monday		
Vernon Massacre✽		
8:00	8:00	8:00
9:00	9:00	9:00
10:00	10:00	10:00
11:00	11:00	11:00
12:00	12:00	12:00
1:00	1:00	1:00
2:00	2:00	2:00
3:00	3:00	3:00
4:00	4:00	4:00
5:00	5:00	5:00
6:00	6:00	6:00
EVENING	EVENING	EVENING
To Do	To Do	To Do

MAY						
S	M	T	W	T	F	S
						1
2	3	4	5	6	7	8
9	10	11	12	13	14	15
16	17	18	19	20	21	22
23	24	25	26	27	28	29
30	31					

2010

8 THURSDAY | 9 FRIDAY | 10 SATURDAY

8:00 | 8:00
9:00 | 9:00
10:00 | 10:00
11:00 | 11:00
12:00 | 12:00

11 SUNDAY
Yom HaSho'ah

1:00 | 1:00
2:00 | 2:00
3:00 | 3:00
4:00 | 4:00
5:00 | 5:00
6:00 | 6:00

NOTES

EVENING | EVENING

* On April 5, 1996, Rajwar Gakhal was killed with eight members of her family in Vernon, BC, by her ex-husband. The Vernon Massacre commemorates Rajwar and all other women who are victims of male violence.

TO DO | TO DO

APRIL

APRIL
S M T W T F S
            1 2 3
 4 5 6 7 8 9 10
11 12 13 14 15 16 17
18 19 20 21 22 23 24
25 26 27 28 29 30

12 MONDAY	*13* TUESDAY	*14* WEDNESDAY ●
	Vaisakhi	
8:00	8:00	8:00
9:00	9:00	9:00
10:00	10:00	10:00
11:00	11:00	11:00
12:00	12:00	12:00
1:00	1:00	1:00
2:00	2:00	2:00
3:00	3:00	3:00
4:00	4:00	4:00
5:00	5:00	5:00
6:00	6:00	6:00
Evening	Evening	Evening
To Do	To Do	To Do

MAY

S	M	T	W	T	F	S
						1
2	3	4	5	6	7	8
9	10	11	12	13	14	15
16	17	18	19	20	21	22
23	24	25	26	27	28	29
30	31					

2010

15 THURSDAY	16 FRIDAY	17 SATURDAY
8:00	8:00	
9:00	9:00	
10:00	10:00	
11:00	11:00	
12:00	12:00	**18 SUNDAY**
1:00	1:00	
2:00	2:00	
3:00	3:00	
4:00	4:00	
5:00	5:00	
6:00	6:00	NOTES
Evening	Evening	
To Do	To Do	

APRIL

APRIL

S	M	T	W	T	F	S
				1	2	3
4	5	6	7	8	9	10
11	12	13	14	15	16	17
18	19	20	21	22	23	24
25	26	27	28	29	30	

19 MONDAY	*20* TUESDAY	*21* WEDNESDAY ☾
8:00	8:00	8:00
9:00	9:00	9:00
10:00	10:00	10:00
11:00	11:00	11:00
12:00	12:00	12:00
1:00	1:00	1:00
2:00	2:00	2:00
3:00	3:00	3:00
4:00	4:00	4:00
5:00	5:00	5:00
6:00	6:00	6:00
Evening	Evening	Evening
To Do	To Do	To Do

MAY

S	M	T	W	T	F	S
						1
2	3	4	5	6	7	8
9	10	11	12	13	14	15
16	17	18	19	20	21	22
23	24	25	26	27	28	29
30	31					

2010

22 THURSDAY	23 FRIDAY	24 SATURDAY
Earth Day		
8:00	8:00	
9:00	9:00	
10:00	10:00	
11:00	11:00	
12:00	12:00	**25 SUNDAY**
1:00	1:00	
2:00	2:00	
3:00	3:00	
4:00	4:00	
5:00	5:00	
6:00	6:00	**NOTES**
EVENING	EVENING	
To Do	To Do	

APRIL

APRIL
S M T W T F S
          1 2 3
4 5 6 7 8 9 10
11 12 13 14 15 16 17
18 19 20 21 22 23 24
25 26 27 28 29 30

26 MONDAY	27 TUESDAY	28 WEDNESDAY ○
		Theravadin New Year
8:00	8:00	8:00
9:00	9:00	9:00
10:00	10:00	10:00
11:00	11:00	11:00
12:00	12:00	12:00
1:00	1:00	1:00
2:00	2:00	2:00
3:00	3:00	3:00
4:00	4:00	4:00
5:00	5:00	5:00
6:00	6:00	6:00
Evening	Evening	Evening
To Do	To Do	To Do

MAY

S	M	T	W	T	F	S
						1
2	3	4	5	6	7	8
9	10	11	12	13	14	15
16	17	18	19	20	21	22
23	24	25	26	27	28	29
30	31					

2010

29 THURSDAY	30 FRIDAY	N O T E S

MAY

▽

JEANNIE AS FRIDA KAHLO

Elaine Brière

Mexican artist Frida Kahlo used the power of art to speak out against injustices of her time. I took this photograph of Jeannie Kamins dressed as Frida Kahlo at a demonstration outside the Vancouver Art Gallery on June 14, 2002. This was one in a series of demonstrations against severe cuts to social services and education made by Gordon Campbell's Liberal government. Extravagant preparations for the coming 2010 Winter Olympics offer a sharp contrast to BC's persistent poverty and homelessness.

Jeannie began her career as a fabric artist, and has branched out into writing, painting, curating, public and performance art. Her subjects are family life, portraits and political issues; she has curated two national exhibitions dealing with censorship in the arts.

MONTH-AT-A-GLANCE PLANNER

			MAY			
SUNDAY	MONDAY	TUESDAY	WEDNESDAY	THURSDAY	FRIDAY	SATURDAY
						1
2	*3*	*4*	*5*	☾ *6*	*7*	*8*
9	*10*	*11*	*12*	● *13*	*14*	*15*
16	*17*	*18*	*19*	☽ *20*	*21*	*22*
23 / *30*	*24* / *31*	*25*	*26*	○ *27*	*28*	*29*

MAY 2010

PROJECTS	TO DO LIST	1	SATURDAY

May Day/Beltane

| 2 | SUNDAY |

NOTES

MAY

	M A Y
	S M T W T F S
	1
	2 3 4 5 6 7 8
	9 10 11 12 13 14 15
	16 17 18 19 20 21 22
	23 24 25 26 27 28 29
	30 31

3 MONDAY	*4* TUESDAY	*5* WEDNESDAY
World Press Freedom Day (UN)		
8:00	8:00	8:00
9:00	9:00	9:00
10:00	10:00	10:00
11:00	11:00	11:00
12:00	12:00	12:00
1:00	1:00	1:00
2:00	2:00	2:00
3:00	3:00	3:00
4:00	4:00	4:00
5:00	5:00	5:00
6:00	6:00	6:00
EVENING	EVENING	EVENING
To Do	To Do	To Do

JUNE

S	M	T	W	T	F	S
		1	2	3	4	5
6	7	8	9	10	11	12
13	14	15	16	17	18	19
20	21	22	23	24	25	26
27	28	29	30			

2010

6 THURSDAY	7 FRIDAY	8 SATURDAY
8:00	8:00	
9:00	9:00	
10:00	10:00	
11:00	11:00	
12:00	12:00	**9 SUNDAY**
1:00	1:00	*Mother's Day*
2:00	2:00	
3:00	3:00	
4:00	4:00	
5:00	5:00	
6:00	6:00	**NOTES**
EVENING	EVENING	
To Do	To Do	

MAY

	M A Y
	S M T W T F S
	1
	2 3 4 5 6 7 8
	9 10 11 12 13 14 15
	16 17 18 19 20 21 22
	23 24 25 26 27 28 29
	30 31

10 MONDAY	11 TUESDAY	12 WEDNESDAY
8:00	8:00	8:00
9:00	9:00	9:00
10:00	10:00	10:00
11:00	11:00	11:00
12:00	12:00	12:00
1:00	1:00	1:00
2:00	2:00	2:00
3:00	3:00	3:00
4:00	4:00	4:00
5:00	5:00	5:00
6:00	6:00	6:00
Evening	Evening	Evening
To Do	To Do	To Do

JUNE						
S	M	T	W	T	F	S
		1	2	3	4	5
6	7	8	9	10	11	12
13	14	15	16	17	18	19
20	21	22	23	24	25	26
27	28	29	30			

2010

13 THURSDAY ●	14 FRIDAY	15 SATURDAY
8:00	8:00	
9:00	9:00	
10:00	10:00	
11:00	11:00	
12:00	12:00	**16 SUNDAY**
1:00	1:00	
2:00	2:00	
3:00	3:00	
4:00	4:00	
5:00	5:00	
6:00	6:00	NOTES
Evening	Evening	
To Do	To Do	

MAY

MAY
S M T W T F S
1
2 3 4 5 6 7 8
9 10 11 12 13 14 15
16 17 18 19 20 21 22
23 24 25 26 27 28 29
30 31

17 MONDAY	18 TUESDAY	19 WEDNESDAY
	Eve of Shavuot	
8:00	8:00	8:00
9:00	9:00	9:00
10:00	10:00	10:00
11:00	11:00	11:00
12:00	12:00	12:00
1:00	1:00	1:00
2:00	2:00	2:00
3:00	3:00	3:00
4:00	4:00	4:00
5:00	5:00	5:00
6:00	6:00	6:00
Evening	Evening	Evening
To Do	To Do	To Do

JUNE

S	M	T	W	T	F	S
		1	2	3	4	5
6	7	8	9	10	11	12
13	14	15	16	17	18	19
20	21	22	23	24	25	26
27	28	29	30			

2010

20 THURSDAY ☽	21 FRIDAY	22 SATURDAY
8:00	8:00	
9:00	9:00	
10:00	10:00	
11:00	11:00	
12:00	12:00	**23 SUNDAY**
1:00	1:00	
2:00	2:00	
3:00	3:00	
4:00	4:00	
5:00	5:00	
6:00	6:00	**NOTES**
Evening	Evening	
To Do	To Do	

MAY

MAY
S M T W T F S
1
2 3 4 5 6 7 8
9 10 11 12 13 14 15
16 17 18 19 20 21 22
23 24 25 26 27 28 29
30 31

24 MONDAY	25 TUESDAY	26 WEDNESDAY
Victoria Day		
8:00	8:00	8:00
9:00	9:00	9:00
10:00	10:00	10:00
11:00	11:00	11:00
12:00	12:00	12:00
1:00	1:00	1:00
2:00	2:00	2:00
3:00	3:00	3:00
4:00	4:00	4:00
5:00	5:00	5:00
6:00	6:00	6:00
Evening	Evening	Evening
To Do	To Do	To Do

JUNE

S	M	T	W	T	F	S
		1	2	3	4	5
6	7	8	9	10	11	12
13	14	15	16	17	18	19
20	21	22	23	24	25	26
27	28	29	30			

2010

27 THURSDAY
Visakha Puja

28 FRIDAY

29 SATURDAY

Thursday	Friday
8:00	8:00
9:00	9:00
10:00	10:00
11:00	11:00
12:00	12:00
1:00	1:00
2:00	2:00
3:00	3:00
4:00	4:00
5:00	5:00
6:00	6:00
Evening	Evening
To Do	To Do

30 SUNDAY

NOTES

MAY

M A Y						
S	M	T	W	T	F	S
						1
2	3	4	5	6	7	8
9	10	11	12	13	14	15
16	17	18	19	20	21	22
23	24	25	26	27	28	29
30	31					

31 MONDAY — NOTES

Memorial Day (US)

8:00

9:00

10:00

11:00

12:00

1:00

2:00

3:00

4:00

5:00

6:00

Evening

To Do

JUNE

S	M	T	W	T	F	S
		1	2	3	4	5
6	7	8	9	10	11	12
13	14	15	16	17	18	19
20	21	22	23	24	25	26
27	28	29	30			

2010

NOTES

JUNE

▽

MUSE

Ewa Monika Zebrowski

This is a photo of my stepdaughter, Talya, a writer and an actress. My photographs of her are always emotionally charged and evocative. I have known Talya since she was seven years old. Initially our relationship was fraught with conflict, but, with time, we found common ground. Being an actress, Talya understands the nuances of gesture and expression.

    This particular portrait was inspired by the work of the British photographer, Julia Margaret Cameron (1815-1879), someone whose work I have long admired. Cameron began photographing late in life after receiving a camera as a gift from her children. She photographed friends and family, people close to her, producing many evocative, timeless portraits, at once ephemeral and poetic.

MONTH-AT-A-GLANCE PLANNER

JUNE

SUNDAY	MONDAY	TUESDAY	WEDNESDAY	THURSDAY	FRIDAY	SATURDAY
		1	2	3	☽ 4	5
6	7	8	9	10	11	● 12
13	14	15	16	17	18	☾ 19
20	21	22	23	24	25	○ 26
27	28	29	30			

JUNE 2010

ONGOING PROJECTS	DUE BY

TO DO LIST

JUNE

JUNE
S M T W T F S
           1 2 3 4 5
6 7 8 9 10 11 12
13 14 15 16 17 18 19
20 21 22 23 24 25 26
27 28 29 30

NOTES	1 TUESDAY	2 WEDNESDAY
	8:00	8:00
	9:00	9:00
	10:00	10:00
	11:00	11:00
	12:00	12:00
	1:00	1:00
	2:00	2:00
	3:00	3:00
	4:00	4:00
	5:00	5:00
	6:00	6:00
	Evening	Evening
	To Do	To Do

JULY

S	M	T	W	T	F	S
				1	2	3
4	5	6	7	8	9	10
11	12	13	14	15	16	17
18	19	20	21	22	23	24
25	26	27	28	29	30	31

2010

3 THURSDAY | 4 FRIDAY ☾ | 5 SATURDAY

Thursday	Friday
8:00	8:00
9:00	9:00
10:00	10:00
11:00	11:00
12:00	12:00
1:00	1:00
2:00	2:00
3:00	3:00
4:00	4:00
5:00	5:00
6:00	6:00
Evening	Evening
To Do	To Do

6 SUNDAY

NOTES

JUNE

JUNE
S M T W T F S
            1 2 3 4 5
6 7 8 9 10 11 12
13 14 15 16 17 18 19
20 21 22 23 24 25 26
27 28 29 30

7 MONDAY	8 TUESDAY	9 WEDNESDAY
8:00	8:00	8:00
9:00	9:00	9:00
10:00	10:00	10:00
11:00	11:00	11:00
12:00	12:00	12:00
1:00	1:00	1:00
2:00	2:00	2:00
3:00	3:00	3:00
4:00	4:00	4:00
5:00	5:00	5:00
6:00	6:00	6:00
Evening	Evening	Evening
To Do	To Do	To Do

JULY

S	M	T	W	T	F	S
				1	2	3
4	5	6	7	8	9	10
11	12	13	14	15	16	17
18	19	20	21	22	23	24
25	26	27	28	29	30	31

2010

10 THURSDAY	11 FRIDAY	12 SATURDAY ●
8:00	8:00	
9:00	9:00	
10:00	10:00	
11:00	11:00	
12:00	12:00	**13 SUNDAY**
1:00	1:00	
2:00	2:00	
3:00	3:00	
4:00	4:00	
5:00	5:00	
6:00	6:00	**NOTES**
Evening	Evening	
To Do	To Do	

JUNE

JUNE
S M T W T F S
                1 2 3 4 5
 6 7 8 9 10 11 12
13 14 15 16 17 18 19
20 21 22 23 24 25 26
27 28 29 30

14 MONDAY	*15* TUESDAY	*16* WEDNESDAY
8:00	8:00	8:00
9:00	9:00	9:00
10:00	10:00	10:00
11:00	11:00	11:00
12:00	12:00	12:00
1:00	1:00	1:00
2:00	2:00	2:00
3:00	3:00	3:00
4:00	4:00	4:00
5:00	5:00	5:00
6:00	6:00	6:00
Evening	Evening	Evening
To Do	To Do	To Do

JULY

S	M	T	W	T	F	S
				1	2	3
4	5	6	7	8	9	10
11	12	13	14	15	16	17
18	19	20	21	22	23	24
25	26	27	28	29	30	31

2010

17 THURSDAY | 18 FRIDAY | 19 SATURDAY ☽

Pride Week Begins (Toronto)

Thursday	Friday
8:00	8:00
9:00	9:00
10:00	10:00
11:00	11:00
12:00	12:00
1:00	1:00
2:00	2:00
3:00	3:00
4:00	4:00
5:00	5:00
6:00	6:00
EVENING	EVENING
To Do	To Do

20 SUNDAY

Father's Day

NOTES

JUNE

JUNE
S M T W T F S
          1 2 3 4 5
6 7 8 9 10 11 12
13 14 15 16 17 18 19
20 21 22 23 24 25 26
27 28 29 30

21 MONDAY	22 TUESDAY	23 WEDNESDAY
National Aboriginal Day		
Summer Solstice		
8:00	8:00	8:00
9:00	9:00	9:00
10:00	10:00	10:00
11:00	11:00	11:00
12:00	12:00	12:00
1:00	1:00	1:00
2:00	2:00	2:00
3:00	3:00	3:00
4:00	4:00	4:00
5:00	5:00	5:00
6:00	6:00	6:00
EVENING	EVENING	EVENING
TO DO	TO DO	TO DO

JULY

S	M	T	W	T	F	S
				1	2	3
4	5	6	7	8	9	10
11	12	13	14	15	16	17
18	19	20	21	22	23	24
25	26	27	28	29	30	31

2010

24 THURSDAY
St. Jean Baptiste Day

25 FRIDAY

26 SATURDAY
Partial Lunar Eclipse

Thursday	Friday
8:00	8:00
9:00	9:00
10:00	10:00
11:00	11:00
12:00	12:00
1:00	1:00
2:00	2:00
3:00	3:00
4:00	4:00
5:00	5:00
6:00	6:00
Evening	Evening
To Do	To Do

27 SUNDAY

NOTES

JUNE

	JUNE
	S M T W T F S
	1 2 3 4 5
	6 7 8 9 10 11 12
	13 14 15 16 17 18 19
	20 21 22 23 24 25 26
	27 28 29 30

28 MONDAY	29 TUESDAY	30 WEDNESDAY
8:00	8:00	8:00
9:00	9:00	9:00
10:00	10:00	10:00
11:00	11:00	11:00
12:00	12:00	12:00
1:00	1:00	1:00
2:00	2:00	2:00
3:00	3:00	3:00
4:00	4:00	4:00
5:00	5:00	5:00
6:00	6:00	6:00
Evening	Evening	Evening
To Do	To Do	To Do

		JULY				
S	M	T W	T	F	S
				1	2	3
4	5	6 7	8	9	10
11	12	13 14	15	16	17
18	19	20 21	22	23	24
25	26	27 28	29	30	31

2010

NOTES

JULY

▽

SONDA TURNER NAMPIJINPA

Lynn Murray

Darwin, Australia. Sonda Turner Nampijinpa was sitting on the ground engrossed in her work; I was instantly intrigued. Her painting was so clear and beautiful, expressing her feeling of oneness with her environment. She smiled, giving me permission to take her photograph. An Australian family stopped, became absorbed by her work, and finally said they would like to buy it.

Turner Nampijinpa's work is highly valued, and she has been exhibited all over Australia. She works on one painting in front of the bookstore in Darwin for a week, sells a piece, and then goes home to the bush. The bookstore owner took me upstairs to see other canvasses by Sonda Turner Nampijinpa; a beautiful painting four feet high by ten feet long sold for $15,000. I would have loved to buy it.

MONTH-AT-A-GLANCE PLANNER

JULY

SUNDAY	MONDAY	TUESDAY	WEDNESDAY	THURSDAY	FRIDAY	SATURDAY
				1	2	3
☾ 4	5	6	7	8	9	10
● 11	12	13	14	15	16	17
☽ 18	19	20	21	22	23	24
○ 25	26	27	28	29	30	31

JULY *2010*

1	THURSDAY	2	FRIDAY	3	SATURDAY
	Canada Day				

8:00		8:00	
9:00		9:00	
10:00		10:00	
11:00		11:00	
12:00		12:00	

4	SUNDAY ☾
	Independence Day (US)

1:00		1:00
2:00		2:00
3:00		3:00
4:00		4:00
5:00		5:00
6:00		6:00

NOTES

EVENING

EVENING

To Do

To Do

JULY

J U L Y
S M T W T F S
1 2 3
4 5 6 7 8 9 10
11 12 13 14 15 16 17
18 19 20 21 22 23 24
25 26 27 28 29 30 31

5 MONDAY	*6* TUESDAY	*7* WEDNESDAY
8:00	8:00	8:00
9:00	9:00	9:00
10:00	10:00	10:00
11:00	11:00	11:00
12:00	12:00	12:00
1:00	1:00	1:00
2:00	2:00	2:00
3:00	3:00	3:00
4:00	4:00	4:00
5:00	5:00	5:00
6:00	6:00	6:00
EVENING	EVENING	EVENING
TO DO	TO DO	TO DO

AUGUST

S	M	T	W	T	F	S
1	2	3	4	5	6	7
8	9	10	11	12	13	14
15	16	17	18	19	20	21
22	23	24	25	26	27	28
29	30	31				

2010

8 THURSDAY	*9* FRIDAY	*10* SATURDAY
8:00	8:00	
9:00	9:00	
10:00	10:00	
11:00	11:00	
12:00	12:00	*11* SUNDAY ●
1:00	1:00	*Total Solar Eclipse*
2:00	2:00	
3:00	3:00	
4:00	4:00	
5:00	5:00	
6:00	6:00	NOTES
Evening	Evening	
To Do	To Do	

JULY

	J U L Y					
S	M	T	W	T	F	S
			1	2	3
4	5	6	7	8	9	10
11	12	13	14	15	16	17
18	19	20	21	22	23	24
25	26	27	28	29	30	31

12 MONDAY	*13* TUESDAY	*14* WEDNESDAY
8:00	8:00	8:00
9:00	9:00	9:00
10:00	10:00	10:00
11:00	11:00	11:00
12:00	12:00	12:00
1:00	1:00	1:00
2:00	2:00	2:00
3:00	3:00	3:00
4:00	4:00	4:00
5:00	5:00	5:00
6:00	6:00	6:00
Evening	Evening	Evening
To Do	To Do	To Do

AUGUST						
S	M	T	W	T	F	S
1	2	3	4	5	6	7
8	9	10	11	12	13	14
15	16	17	18	19	20	21
22	23	24	25	26	27	28
29	30	31				

2010

15 THURSDAY	16 FRIDAY	17 SATURDAY
8:00	8:00	
9:00	9:00	
10:00	10:00	
11:00	11:00	
12:00	12:00	**18 SUNDAY**
1:00	1:00	
2:00	2:00	
3:00	3:00	
4:00	4:00	
5:00	5:00	
6:00	6:00	N O T E S
EVENING	EVENING	
To Do	To Do	

JULY

JULY
S M T W T F S
1 2 3
4 5 6 7 8 9 10
11 12 13 14 15 16 17
18 19 20 21 22 23 24
25 26 27 28 29 30 31

19 MONDAY	*20* TUESDAY	*21* WEDNESDAY
8:00	8:00	8:00
9:00	9:00	9:00
10:00	10:00	10:00
11:00	11:00	11:00
12:00	12:00	12:00
1:00	1:00	1:00
2:00	2:00	2:00
3:00	3:00	3:00
4:00	4:00	4:00
5:00	5:00	5:00
6:00	6:00	6:00
Evening	Evening	Evening
To Do	To Do	To Do

AUGUST

S	M	T	W	T	F	S
1	2	3	4	5	6	7
8	9	10	11	12	13	14
15	16	17	18	19	20	21
22	23	24	25	26	27	28
29	30	31				

2010

22 THURSDAY	23 FRIDAY	24 SATURDAY
8:00	8:00	
9:00	9:00	
10:00	10:00	
11:00	11:00	
12:00	12:00	**25 SUNDAY** ○
1:00	1:00	
2:00	2:00	
3:00	3:00	
4:00	4:00	
5:00	5:00	
6:00	6:00	NOTES
EVENING	EVENING	
To Do	To Do	

JULY

	JULY
	S M T W T F S
	1 2 3
	4 5 6 7 8 9 10
	11 12 13 14 15 16 17
	18 19 20 21 22 23 24
	25 26 27 28 29 30 31

26 MONDAY	27 TUESDAY	28 WEDNESDAY
Asalha Puja		
8:00	8:00	8:00
9:00	9:00	9:00
10:00	10:00	10:00
11:00	11:00	11:00
12:00	12:00	12:00
1:00	1:00	1:00
2:00	2:00	2:00
3:00	3:00	3:00
4:00	4:00	4:00
5:00	5:00	5:00
6:00	6:00	6:00
EVENING	EVENING	EVENING
TO DO	TO DO	TO DO

AUGUST

S	M	T	W	T	F	S
1	2	3	4	5	6	7
8	9	10	11	12	13	14
15	16	17	18	19	20	21
22	23	24	25	26	27	28
29	30	31				

2010

29 THURSDAY	30 FRIDAY	31 SATURDAY
8:00	8:00	
9:00	9:00	
10:00	10:00	
11:00	11:00	
12:00	12:00	NOTES
1:00	1:00	
2:00	2:00	
3:00	3:00	
4:00	4:00	
5:00	5:00	
6:00	6:00	
Evening	Evening	
To Do	To Do	

AUGUST

▽

TRISH WITH TEXTILE WORK

Laura Watt

This photograph of my mother was taken in her garden. Despite the warm summer day, she was working with a heavy textile piece on her lap, hooking a rug depicting her mother. Although we come from a long line of creative women, only the last few generations have referred to themselves as artists. Women have always been creative, yet in the past textile works have been considered merely practical objects. But the quilts and rugs serve much more purpose, documenting experience, sharing stories, preserving history — artistically. Women continue to congregate in guilds and collectives, in church basements, living rooms, studios and gardens, as they have for generations, stitching their lives into art.

MONTH-AT-A-GLANCE PLANNER

AUGUST

Sunday	Monday	Tuesday	Wednesday	Thursday	Friday	Saturday
1	2	☾ 3	4	5	6	7
8	● 9	10	11	12	13	14
15	☽ 16	17	18	19	20	21
22	23	○ 24	25	26	27	28
29	30	31				

AUGUST *2010*

PROJECTS	TO DO LIST	*1*	SUNDAY

NOTES

AUGUST

AUGUST
S M T W T F S
1 2 3 4 5 6 7
8 9 10 11 12 13 14
15 16 17 18 19 20 21
22 23 24 25 26 27 28
29 30 31

2 MONDAY	3 TUESDAY ☽	4 WEDNESDAY
Civic Holiday (Canada)		
8:00	8:00	8:00
9:00	9:00	9:00
10:00	10:00	10:00
11:00	11:00	11:00
12:00	12:00	12:00
1:00	1:00	1:00
2:00	2:00	2:00
3:00	3:00	3:00
4:00	4:00	4:00
5:00	5:00	5:00
6:00	6:00	6:00
Evening	Evening	Evening
To Do	To Do	To Do

SEPTEMBER

S	M	T	W	T	F	S
			1	2	3	4
5	6	7	8	9	10	11
12	13	14	15	16	17	18
19	20	21	22	23	24	25
26	27	28	29	30		

2010

5 THURSDAY	6 FRIDAY	7 SATURDAY
8:00	8:00	
9:00	9:00	
10:00	10:00	
11:00	11:00	
12:00	12:00	**8 SUNDAY**
1:00	1:00	
2:00	2:00	
3:00	3:00	
4:00	4:00	
5:00	5:00	
6:00	6:00	**NOTES**
Evening	Evening	
To Do	To Do	

AUGUST

AUGUST
S M T W T F S
1 2 3 4 5 6 7
8 9 10 11 12 13 14
15 16 17 18 19 20 21
22 23 24 25 26 27 28
29 30 31

9 MONDAY ●	*10* TUESDAY	*11* WEDNESDAY
		Ramadan begins
8:00	8:00	8:00
9:00	9:00	9:00
10:00	10:00	10:00
11:00	11:00	11:00
12:00	12:00	12:00
1:00	1:00	1:00
2:00	2:00	2:00
3:00	3:00	3:00
4:00	4:00	4:00
5:00	5:00	5:00
6:00	6:00	6:00
EVENING	EVENING	EVENING
TO DO	TO DO	TO DO

SEPTEMBER

S	M	T	W	T	F	S
			1	2	3	4
5	6	7	8	9	10	11
12	13	14	15	16	17	18
19	20	21	22	23	24	25
26	27	28	29	30		

2010

12 THURSDAY	13 FRIDAY	14 SATURDAY
8:00	8:00	
9:00	9:00	
10:00	10:00	
11:00	11:00	
12:00	12:00	**15 SUNDAY**
1:00	1:00	
2:00	2:00	
3:00	3:00	
4:00	4:00	
5:00	5:00	
6:00	6:00	NOTES
Evening	Evening	
To Do	To Do	

AUGUST

AUGUST
S M T W T F S
1 2 3 4 5 6 7
8 9 10 11 12 13 14
15 16 17 18 19 20 21
22 23 24 25 26 27 28
29 30 31

16 MONDAY ☽	**17** TUESDAY	**18** WEDNESDAY
8:00	8:00	8:00
9:00	9:00	9:00
10:00	10:00	10:00
11:00	11:00	11:00
12:00	12:00	12:00
1:00	1:00	1:00
2:00	2:00	2:00
3:00	3:00	3:00
4:00	4:00	4:00
5:00	5:00	5:00
6:00	6:00	6:00
Evening	Evening	Evening
To Do	To Do	To Do

SEPTEMBER

S	M	T	W	T	F	S
			1	2	3	4
5	6	7	8	9	10	11
12	13	14	15	16	17	18
19	20	21	22	23	24	25
26	27	28	29	30		

2010

19 THURSDAY	20 FRIDAY	21 SATURDAY
8:00	8:00	
9:00	9:00	
10:00	10:00	
11:00	11:00	
12:00	12:00	**22 SUNDAY**
1:00	1:00	
2:00	2:00	
3:00	3:00	
4:00	4:00	
5:00	5:00	
6:00	6:00	**NOTES**
Evening	Evening	
To Do	To Do	

AUGUST

AUGUST
S M T W T F S
1 2 3 4 5 6 7
8 9 10 11 12 13 14
15 16 17 18 19 20 21
22 23 24 25 26 27 28
29 30 31

23 MONDAY	24 TUESDAY ○	25 WEDNESDAY
	Raksha Bandhan	
8:00	8:00	8:00
9:00	9:00	9:00
10:00	10:00	10:00
11:00	11:00	11:00
12:00	12:00	12:00
1:00	1:00	1:00
2:00	2:00	2:00
3:00	3:00	3:00
4:00	4:00	4:00
5:00	5:00	5:00
6:00	6:00	6:00
Evening	Evening	Evening
To Do	To Do	To Do

SEPTEMBER

S	M	T	W	T	F	S
			1	2	3	4
5	6	7	8	9	10	11
12	13	14	15	16	17	18
19	20	21	22	23	24	25
26	27	28	29	30		

2010

26 THURSDAY	27 FRIDAY	28 SATURDAY
8:00	8:00	
9:00	9:00	
10:00	10:00	
11:00	11:00	
12:00	12:00	**29 SUNDAY**
1:00	1:00	
2:00	2:00	
3:00	3:00	
4:00	4:00	
5:00	5:00	
6:00	6:00	N O T E S
Evening	Evening	
To Do	To Do	

AUGUST

AUGUST

S	M	T	W	T	F	S
1	2	3	4	5	6	7
8	9	10	11	12	13	14
15	16	17	18	19	20	21
22	23	24	25	26	27	28
29	30	31				

30 MONDAY	*31* TUESDAY	NOTES
8:00	8:00	
9:00	9:00	
10:00	10:00	
11:00	11:00	
12:00	12:00	
1:00	1:00	
2:00	2:00	
3:00	3:00	
4:00	4:00	
5:00	5:00	
6:00	6:00	
EVENING	EVENING	
To Do	To Do	

SEPTEMBER

S	M	T	W	T	F	S
			1	2	3	4
5	6	7	8	9	10	11
12	13	14	15	16	17	18
19	20	21	22	23	24	25
26	27	28	29	30		

2010

NOTES

SEPTEMBER

▽

MARY CARTMEL SCULPTING
A MURDER OF CROWS

Louise Abbott

Thirty years ago, artist Mary Cartmel was given some soapstone to sculpt. "Before that, I had only worked with clay," she recalls. "I fell in love with soapstone. I realized that I preferred taking away material, rather than adding material, to create a form."

Happiest in a rural environment, Mary finds inspiration in the wildlife around her. During her long residency in Quebec's Eastern Townships, she has produced sculptures of amphibians, mammals and reptiles. But it is birds that have dominated her work.

On the day that I photographed her, Mary was starting a new avian scupture. Over the ensuing weeks, she transformed the carefully selected Brazilian soapstone into a flock, or "murder," of crows, sleek, dark and mysterious.

MONTH-AT-A-GLANCE PLANNER

SEPTEMBER

Sunday	Monday	Tuesday	Wednesday	Thursday	Friday	Saturday
			☾ 1	2	3	4
5	6	7	● 8	9	10	11
12	13	14	☽ 15	16	17	18
19	20	21	22	○ 23	24	25
26	27	28	29	☾ 30		

SEPTEMBER 2010

ONGOING PROJECTS	DUE BY

TO DO LIST

SEPTEMBER

SEPTEMBER
S M T W T F S
                1 2 3 4
5 6 7 8 9 10 11
12 13 14 15 16 17 18
19 20 21 22 23 24 25
26 27 28 29 30

N O T E S	*1* WEDNESDAY ☾
	8:00
	9:00
	10:00
	11:00
	12:00
	1:00
	2:00
	3:00
	4:00
	5:00
	6:00
	Evening
	To Do

OCTOBER

S	M	T	W	T	F	S
					1	2
3	4	5	6	7	8	9
10	11	12	13	14	15	16
17	18	19	20	21	22	23
24	25	26	27	28	29	30
31						

2010

2 THURSDAY	3 FRIDAY	4 SATURDAY
Sri Krishna Jayanti		
8:00	8:00	
9:00	9:00	
10:00	10:00	
11:00	11:00	
12:00	12:00	**5 SUNDAY**
1:00	1:00	
2:00	2:00	
3:00	3:00	
4:00	4:00	
5:00	5:00	
6:00	6:00	**NOTES**
Evening	Evening	
To Do	To Do	

SEPTEMBER

SEPTEMBER
S M T W T F S
           1 2 3 4
5 6 7 8 9 10 11
12 13 14 15 16 17 18
19 20 21 22 23 24 25
26 27 28 29 30

6 MONDAY	7 TUESDAY	8 WEDNESDAY ●
Labour Day		*Eve of Rosh Hashanah*
8:00	8:00	8:00
9:00	9:00	9:00
10:00	10:00	10:00
11:00	11:00	11:00
12:00	12:00	12:00
1:00	1:00	1:00
2:00	2:00	2:00
3:00	3:00	3:00
4:00	4:00	4:00
5:00	5:00	5:00
6:00	6:00	6:00
EVENING	EVENING	EVENING
To Do	To Do	To Do

OCTOBER

S	M	T	W	T	F	S
					1	2
3	4	5	6	7	8	9
10	11	12	13	14	15	16
17	18	19	20	21	22	23
24	25	26	27	28	29	30
31						

2010

9 THURSDAY	10 FRIDAY	11 SATURDAY
	Eid al-Fitr	*Ganesh Chaturthi*
8:00	8:00	
9:00	9:00	
10:00	10:00	
11:00	11:00	
12:00	12:00	**12 SUNDAY**
1:00	1:00	*Grandparent's Day*
2:00	2:00	
3:00	3:00	
4:00	4:00	
5:00	5:00	
6:00	6:00	N O T E S
EVENING	EVENING	
To Do	To Do	

SEPTEMBER

SEPTEMBER
S M T W T F S
       1 2 3 4
5 6 7 8 9 10 11
12 13 14 15 16 17 18
19 20 21 22 23 24 25
26 27 28 29 30

13 MONDAY	14 TUESDAY	15 WEDNESDAY ☽
8:00	8:00	8:00
9:00	9:00	9:00
10:00	10:00	10:00
11:00	11:00	11:00
12:00	12:00	12:00
1:00	1:00	1:00
2:00	2:00	2:00
3:00	3:00	3:00
4:00	4:00	4:00
5:00	5:00	5:00
6:00	6:00	6:00
Evening	Evening	Evening
To Do	To Do	To Do

OCTOBER

S	M	T	W	T	F	S
					1	2
3	4	5	6	7	8	9
10	11	12	13	14	15	16
17	18	19	20	21	22	23
24	25	26	27	28	29	30
31						

2010

16 THURSDAY

17 FRIDAY
Eve of Yom Kippur

18 SATURDAY

8:00

9:00

10:00

11:00

12:00

19 SUNDAY

1:00

2:00

3:00

4:00

5:00

6:00

NOTES

Evening

To Do

SEPTEMBER

SEPTEMBER
S M T W T F S
          1 2 3 4
5 6 7 8 9 10 11
12 13 14 15 16 17 18
19 20 21 22 23 24 25
26 27 28 29 30

20 MONDAY	21 TUESDAY	22 WEDNESDAY
	International Day of Peace	*Eve of Sukkot*
8:00	8:00	8:00
9:00	9:00	9:00
10:00	10:00	10:00
11:00	11:00	11:00
12:00	12:00	12:00
1:00	1:00	1:00
2:00	2:00	2:00
3:00	3:00	3:00
4:00	4:00	4:00
5:00	5:00	5:00
6:00	6:00	6:00
EVENING	EVENING	EVENING
To Do	To Do	To Do

OCTOBER

S	M	T	W	T	F	S
					1	2
3	4	5	6	7	8	9
10	11	12	13	14	15	16
17	18	19	20	21	22	23
24	25	26	27	28	29	30
31

2010

23 THURSDAY ○   **24 FRIDAY**   **25 SATURDAY**

Autumnal Equinox

8:00	8:00
9:00	9:00
10:00	10:00
11:00	11:00
12:00	12:00

26 SUNDAY

1:00	1:00
2:00	2:00
3:00	3:00
4:00	4:00
5:00	5:00
6:00	6:00

NOTES

EVENING   EVENING

TO DO   TO DO

SEPTEMBER

SEPTEMBER
S M T W T F S
           1 2 3 4
 5 6 7 8 9 10 11
12 13 14 15 16 17 18
19 20 21 22 23 24 25
26 27 28 29 30

27 MONDAY	28 TUESDAY	29 WEDNESDAY
8:00	8:00	8:00
9:00	9:00	9:00
10:00	10:00	10:00
11:00	11:00	11:00
12:00	12:00	12:00
1:00	1:00	1:00
2:00	2:00	2:00
3:00	3:00	3:00
4:00	4:00	4:00
5:00	5:00	5:00
6:00	6:00	6:00
EVENING	EVENING	EVENING
To Do	To Do	To Do

OCTOBER
S M T W T F S
                1 2
3 4 5 6 7 8 9
10 11 12 13 14 15 16
17 18 19 20 21 22 23
24 25 26 27 28 29 30
31

2010

30	THURSDAY	☾	N O T E S

8:00	
9:00	
10:00	
11:00	
12:00	
1:00	
2:00	
3:00	
4:00	
5:00	
6:00	
Evening	
To Do	

OCTOBER
▽

WOMEN'S WORDS –
WRITER BARBARA GOWDY

Jill Glessing

Reading and writing was for the men. The "word" was given to man. His writing made our laws. Women's words came through voice — songs sung to children, domestic chatter, whispers, talk to the animals and the fields, old wives tales ...

Now we write words too, and our songs are made visible across paper. We breathe our words, press them into lines, fonts, shapes. We lay our voices down upon the page and send them into the hands and hearts of others.

There was no reason for her to continue working in the nude, not in the afternoon, but she did, out of habit and comfort and on the outside chance that Andrew might be home and looking through his drapes. While she painted, she wondered about her exhibitionism, what it was in her that craved to have a strange man look at her. Of course everyone and everything liked to be looked at to a certain degree, she thought. Flowers, anything that preened or shone, children saying "Look at me!" Some mornings her exhibitionism and Andrew seemed to have nothing at all to do with lust. They were completely display, which was a surrender to what felt like the most fundamental of all desires, which was that one needed to be expressed.

One night Andrew mentioned as

MONTH-AT-A-GLANCE PLANNER

OCTOBER

Sunday	Monday	Tuesday	Wednesday	Thursday	Friday	Saturday
					1	2
3	4	5	6	● 7	8	9
10	11	12	13	☽ 14	15	16
17	18	19	20	21	○ 22	23
24 / 31	25	26	27	28	29	☾ 30

OCTOBER 2010

PROJECTS	1 FRIDAY	2 SATURDAY
	Breast Cancer Awareness Month	
	Women's History Month	
	8:00	
	9:00	
	10:00	
	11:00	
	12:00	3 SUNDAY
	1:00	
	2:00	
TO DO LIST	3:00	
	4:00	
	5:00	
	6:00	NOTES
	EVENING	
	To Do	

OCTOBER

OCTOBER
S M T W T F S
         1 2
3 4 5 6 7 8 9
10 11 12 13 14 15 16
17 18 19 20 21 22 23
24 25 26 27 28 29 30
31

4 MONDAY	*5* TUESDAY	*6* WEDNESDAY
8:00	8:00	8:00
9:00	9:00	9:00
10:00	10:00	10:00
11:00	11:00	11:00
12:00	12:00	12:00
1:00	1:00	1:00
2:00	2:00	2:00
3:00	3:00	3:00
4:00	4:00	4:00
5:00	5:00	5:00
6:00	6:00	6:00
Evening	Evening	Evening
To Do	To Do	To Do

NOVEMBER

S	M	T	W	T	F	S
	1	2	3	4	5	6
7	8	9	10	11	12	13
14	15	16	17	18	19	20
21	22	23	24	25	26	27
28	29	30				

2010

7 THURSDAY ●	8 FRIDAY	9 SATURDAY
8:00	8:00	
9:00	9:00	
10:00	10:00	
11:00	11:00	
12:00	12:00	10 SUNDAY
1:00	1:00	
2:00	2:00	
3:00	3:00	
4:00	4:00	
5:00	5:00	
6:00	6:00	NOTES
Evening	Evening	
To Do	To Do	

OCTOBER

OCTOBER

S	M	T	W	T	F	S
					1	2
3	4	5	6	7	8	9
10	11	12	13	14	15	16
17	18	19	20	21	22	23
24	25	26	27	28	29	30
31						

11 MONDAY | 12 TUESDAY | 13 WEDNESDAY

Thanksgiving Day (Canada)
Columbus Day (US)

11 MONDAY	12 TUESDAY	13 WEDNESDAY
8:00	8:00	8:00
9:00	9:00	9:00
10:00	10:00	10:00
11:00	11:00	11:00
12:00	12:00	12:00
1:00	1:00	1:00
2:00	2:00	2:00
3:00	3:00	3:00
4:00	4:00	4:00
5:00	5:00	5:00
6:00	6:00	6:00
Evening	Evening	Evening
To Do	To Do	To Do

NOVEMBER

S	M	T	W	T	F	S
	1	2	3	4	5	6
7	8	9	10	11	12	13
14	15	16	17	18	19	20
21	22	23	24	25	26	27
28	29	30

2010

14 THURSDAY ☽ | 15 FRIDAY | 16 SATURDAY

World Food Day

Thursday 14
8:00
9:00
10:00
11:00
12:00
1:00
2:00
3:00
4:00
5:00
6:00
Evening
To Do

Friday 15
8:00
9:00
10:00
11:00
12:00
1:00
2:00
3:00
4:00
5:00
6:00
Evening
To Do

17 SUNDAY

NOTES

OCTOBER

OCTOBER
S M T W T F S
           1 2
3 4 5 6 7 8 9
10 11 12 13 14 15 16
17 18 19 20 21 22 23
24 25 26 27 28 29 30
31

18 MONDAY	*19* TUESDAY	*20* WEDNESDAY
Persons Day		
8:00	8:00	8:00
9:00	9:00	9:00
10:00	10:00	10:00
11:00	11:00	11:00
12:00	12:00	12:00
1:00	1:00	1:00
2:00	2:00	2:00
3:00	3:00	3:00
4:00	4:00	4:00
5:00	5:00	5:00
6:00	6:00	6:00
Evening	Evening	Evening
To Do	To Do	To Do

NOVEMBER

S	M	T	W	T	F	S
	1	2	3	4	5	6
7	8	9	10	11	12	13
14	15	16	17	18	19	20
21	22	23	24	25	26	27
28	29	30				

2010

21 THURSDAY

- 8:00
- 9:00
- 10:00
- 11:00
- 12:00
- 1:00
- 2:00
- 3:00
- 4:00
- 5:00
- 6:00

EVENING

To Do

22 FRIDAY ○

- 8:00
- 9:00
- 10:00
- 11:00
- 12:00
- 1:00
- 2:00
- 3:00
- 4:00
- 5:00
- 6:00

EVENING

To Do

23 SATURDAY

24 SUNDAY

United Nations Day

NOTES

* October 18 celebrates the hard work of the "Famous Five" that led to the 1925 Privy Council decision which declared women as persons and therefore eligible to be appointed to the Senate of Canada.

OCTOBER

OCTOBER
S	M	T	W	T	F	S
					1	2
3	4	5	6	7	8	9
10	11	12	13	14	15	16
17	18	19	20	21	22	23
24	25	26	27	28	29	30
31						

25 MONDAY	26 TUESDAY	27 WEDNESDAY
8:00	8:00	8:00
9:00	9:00	9:00
10:00	10:00	10:00
11:00	11:00	11:00
12:00	12:00	12:00
1:00	1:00	1:00
2:00	2:00	2:00
3:00	3:00	3:00
4:00	4:00	4:00
5:00	5:00	5:00
6:00	6:00	6:00
EVENING	EVENING	EVENING
TO DO	TO DO	TO DO

NOVEMBER

S	M	T	W	T	F	S
	1	2	3	4	5	6
7	8	9	10	11	12	13
14	15	16	17	18	19	20
21	22	23	24	25	26	27
28	29	30				

2010

28 THURSDAY	29 FRIDAY	30 SATURDAY ☾
8:00	8:00	
9:00	9:00	
10:00	10:00	
11:00	11:00	
12:00	12:00	**31 SUNDAY**
1:00	1:00	*Halloween*
2:00	2:00	
3:00	3:00	
4:00	4:00	
5:00	5:00	
6:00	6:00	NOTES
EVENING	EVENING	
To Do	To Do	

NOVEMBER

▽

ART ON THE JOB

Mary Louise Chown

My niece Elizabeth is always on the job. She is the young single mother of five-year-old Victoria. She has to earn a living wage, but she has found ingenious ways to work her love of art into her daily grind, and to include her daughter in her workday world. Elizabeth is a true artist. She revels in the beautiful colours and shapes of the city gardens and trees, and she finds unusual forms and structures in ordinary everyday objects. Right now she is exploring these forms and shapes and colours with her camera, and her fused art pieces. By day she works as a furniture stripper and refinisher, and restorer of stained glass. During breaks, Elizabeth works on her art. Her boss lets her come in to work at odd hours, especially when there is no sitter for Victoria. Here she is, working on a Saturday morning, Victoria watching a mini movie on top of the workbench, and occasionally getting into the picture.

MONTH-AT-A-GLANCE PLANNER

NOVEMBER

SUNDAY	MONDAY	TUESDAY	WEDNESDAY	THURSDAY	FRIDAY	SATURDAY
	1	2	3	4	5	● 6
7	8	9	10	11	12	☽ 13
14	15	16	17	18	19	20
○ 21	22	23	24	25	26	27
☾ 28	29	30				

NOVEMBER *2010*

ONGOING PROJECTS   DUE BY

TO DO LIST

NOVEMBER

NOVEMBER
S M T W T F S
      1 2 3 4 5 6
7 8 9 10 11 12 13
14 15 16 17 18 19 20
21 22 23 24 25 26 27
28 29 30

1 MONDAY	*2* TUESDAY	*3* WEDNESDAY
All Saints' Day		
8:00	8:00	8:00
9:00	9:00	9:00
10:00	10:00	10:00
11:00	11:00	11:00
12:00	12:00	12:00
1:00	1:00	1:00
2:00	2:00	2:00
3:00	3:00	3:00
4:00	4:00	4:00
5:00	5:00	5:00
6:00	6:00	6:00
EVENING	EVENING	EVENING
TO DO	TO DO	TO DO

DECEMBER
S M T W T F S
1 2 3 4
5 6 7 8 9 10 11
12 13 14 15 16 17 18
19 20 21 22 23 24 25
26 27 28 29 30 31

2010

4 THURSDAY	*5* FRIDAY	*6* SATURDAY ●
	Diwali	
8:00	8:00	
9:00	9:00	
10:00	10:00	
11:00	11:00	
12:00	12:00	*7* SUNDAY
1:00	1:00	*Daylight Saving Time ends*
2:00	2:00	
3:00	3:00	
4:00	4:00	
5:00	5:00	
6:00	6:00	NOTES
EVENING	EVENING	
TO DO	TO DO	

NOVEMBER

NOVEMBER
S M T W T F S
         1 2 3 4 5 6
7 8 9 10 11 12 13
14 15 16 17 18 19 20
21 22 23 24 25 26 27
28 29 30

8 MONDAY	*9* TUESDAY	*10* WEDNESDAY
8:00	8:00	8:00
9:00	9:00	9:00
10:00	10:00	10:00
11:00	11:00	11:00
12:00	12:00	12:00
1:00	1:00	1:00
2:00	2:00	2:00
3:00	3:00	3:00
4:00	4:00	4:00
5:00	5:00	5:00
6:00	6:00	6:00
EVENING	EVENING	EVENING
To Do	To Do	To Do

DECEMBER
S M T W T F S
       1 2 3 4
5 6 7 8 9 10 11
12 13 14 15 16 17 18
19 20 21 22 23 24 25
26 27 28 29 30 31

2010

11 THURSDAY	12 FRIDAY	13 SATURDAY
Remembrance Day (Canada)	*Birth of Baha'u'llah*	
Veterans Day (US)		
8:00	8:00	
9:00	9:00	
10:00	10:00	
11:00	11:00	
12:00	12:00	**14 SUNDAY**
1:00	1:00	
2:00	2:00	
3:00	3:00	
4:00	4:00	
5:00	5:00	
6:00	6:00	N O T E S
EVENING	EVENING	
To Do	To Do	

NOVEMBER

NOVEMBER
S M T W T F S
         1 2 3 4 5 6
 7 8 9 10 11 12 13
14 15 16 17 18 19 20
21 22 23 24 25 26 27
28 29 30

15 MONDAY	*16* TUESDAY	*17* WEDNESDAY
Hajj begins / Waqf al-Arafa		*Eid al-Adha*
8:00	8:00	8:00
9:00	9:00	9:00
10:00	10:00	10:00
11:00	11:00	11:00
12:00	12:00	12:00
1:00	1:00	1:00
2:00	2:00	2:00
3:00	3:00	3:00
4:00	4:00	4:00
5:00	5:00	5:00
6:00	6:00	6:00
EVENING	EVENING	EVENING
To Do	To Do	To Do

DECEMBER						
S	M	T	W	T	F	S
			1	2	3	4
5	6	7	8	9	10	11
12	13	14	15	16	17	18
19	20	21	22	23	24	25
26	27	28	29	30	31	

2010

18 THURSDAY	19 FRIDAY	20 SATURDAY
8:00	8:00	
9:00	9:00	
10:00	10:00	
11:00	11:00	
12:00	12:00	**21 SUNDAY** ○
1:00	1:00	
2:00	2:00	
3:00	3:00	
4:00	4:00	
5:00	5:00	
6:00	6:00	NOTES
EVENING	EVENING	
To Do	To Do	

NOVEMBER

NOVEMBER

S	M	T	W	T	F	S
	1	2	3	4	5	6
7	8	9	10	11	12	13
14	15	16	17	18	19	20
21	22	23	24	25	26	27
28	29	30				

22 MONDAY	23 TUESDAY	24 WEDNESDAY
8:00	8:00	8:00
9:00	9:00	9:00
10:00	10:00	10:00
11:00	11:00	11:00
12:00	12:00	12:00
1:00	1:00	1:00
2:00	2:00	2:00
3:00	3:00	3:00
4:00	4:00	4:00
5:00	5:00	5:00
6:00	6:00	6:00
Evening	Evening	Evening
To Do	To Do	To Do

DECEMBER
S M T W T F S
1 2 3 4
5 6 7 8 9 10 11
12 13 14 15 16 17 18
19 20 21 22 23 24 25
26 27 28 29 30 31

2010

25	THURSDAY	26	FRIDAY	27	SATURDAY

International Day for the Elimination of Violence Against Women

8:00	*Thanksgiving Day (US)*	8:00	
9:00		9:00	
10:00		10:00	
11:00		11:00	
12:00		12:00	

28	SUNDAY

First Sunday of Advent

1:00		1:00	
2:00		2:00	
3:00		3:00	
4:00		4:00	
5:00		5:00	
6:00		6:00	

NOTES

EVENING

EVENING

TO DO

TO DO

NOVEMBER

NOVEMBER
S M T W T F S
1 2 3 4 5 6
7 8 9 10 11 12 13
14 15 16 17 18 19 20
21 22 23 24 25 26 27
28 29 30

29 MONDAY	*30* TUESDAY	N O T E S
8:00	8:00	
9:00	9:00	
10:00	10:00	
11:00	11:00	
12:00	12:00	
1:00	1:00	
2:00	2:00	
3:00	3:00	
4:00	4:00	
5:00	5:00	
6:00	6:00	
Evening	Evening	
To Do	To Do	

DECEMBER
S M T W T F S
          1 2 3 4
 5 6 7 8 9 10 11
12 13 14 15 16 17 18
19 20 21 22 23 24 25
26 27 28 29 30 31

NOTES

DECEMBER

▽

ANNE

Sheilagh Ethne O'Leary

The human anatomy has always fascinated me. When I was little, I spent hours flipping through the pages of my mother's nursing anatomy book. I have vivid memories of the beautifully coloured drawings on transparencies that flipped, one over the other, to give dimension to its exploration of the human body. In a climate where Catholic schoolgirls squeezed in and out of uniforms after gym without ever revealing an inch of exposed skin, it was my mother's belief that the human body is beautiful, and not to be feared or ashamed of, that set the seed for my later study of the human form.

While I love the aesthetics of the human form, what really interests me is the possibility of revealing what lies beneath the layers of the skin. So I focus my work on an exploration of human nature, both the light and the dark of it — love and empathy, as well as cruelty and violence.

My experience growing up in Newfoundland has been a driving force in my work; living here, one is very much on the edge. There is no hiding in this spare landscape — the geography forces us out and exposes us. It's fantastic and terrible, and we are at once fragile and strong. This tension between opposites is always present, and I try to bring that tension into my work.

MONTH-AT-A-GLANCE PLANNER

DECEMBER

SUNDAY	MONDAY	TUESDAY	WEDNESDAY	THURSDAY	FRIDAY	SATURDAY
			1	2	3	4
● 5	6	7	8	9	10	11
12	☽ 13	14	15	16	17	18
19	20	○ 21	22	23	24	25
26	☾ 27	28	29	30	31	

DECEMBER 2010

ONGOING PROJECTS	DUE BY

TO DO LIST

DECEMBER

DECEMBER
S M T W T F S
              1 2 3 4
5 6 7 8 9 10 11
12 13 14 15 16 17 18
19 20 21 22 23 24 25
26 27 28 29 30 31

NOTES	*1* **WEDNESDAY**
	World AIDS Day
	Eve of Hanukkah
	8:00
	9:00
	10:00
	11:00
	12:00
	1:00
	2:00
	3:00
	4:00
	5:00
	6:00
	EVENING
	To Do

JANUARY						
S	M	T	W	T	F	S
						1
2	3	4	5	6	7	8
9	10	11	12	13	14	15
16	17	18	19	20	21	22
23	24	25	26	27	28	29
30	31					

2010

2 THURSDAY | 3 FRIDAY | 4 SATURDAY

International Day of Persons with Disabilities

2 THURSDAY	3 FRIDAY
8:00	8:00
9:00	9:00
10:00	10:00
11:00	11:00
12:00	12:00
1:00	1:00
2:00	2:00
3:00	3:00
4:00	4:00
5:00	5:00
6:00	6:00
Evening	Evening
To Do	To Do

5 SUNDAY ●

NOTES

DECEMBER

DECEMBER
S M T W T F S
              1 2 3 4
5 6 7 8 9 10 11
12 13 14 15 16 17 18
19 20 21 22 23 24 25
26 27 28 29 30 31

6 MONDAY	7 TUESDAY	8 WEDNESDAY
National Day of Remembrance & Action on Violence Against Women	*Al-Hijra*	
8:00	8:00	8:00
9:00	9:00	9:00
10:00	10:00	10:00
11:00	11:00	11:00
12:00	12:00	12:00
1:00	1:00	1:00
2:00	2:00	2:00
3:00	3:00	3:00
4:00	4:00	4:00
5:00	5:00	5:00
6:00	6:00	6:00
EVENING	EVENING	EVENING
To Do	To Do	To Do

JANUARY

S	M	T	W	T	F	S
						1
2	3	4	5	6	7	8
9	10	11	12	13	14	15
16	17	18	19	20	21	22
23	24	25	26	27	28	29
30	31					

2010

9 THURSDAY | 10 FRIDAY | 11 SATURDAY

Human Rights Day

THURSDAY	FRIDAY
8:00	8:00
9:00	9:00
10:00	10:00
11:00	11:00
12:00	12:00
1:00	1:00
2:00	2:00
3:00	3:00
4:00	4:00
5:00	5:00
6:00	6:00
Evening	Evening
To Do	To Do

12 SUNDAY

NOTES

✷ December 6 commemorates the mass murder of fourteen young women at the École Polytechnique in Montreal in 1989.

DECEMBER

DECEMBER

S	M	T	W	T	F	S
			1	2	3	4
5	6	7	8	9	10	11
12	13	14	15	16	17	18
19	20	21	22	23	24	25
26	27	28	29	30	31	

13 MONDAY ☽ | 14 TUESDAY | 15 WEDNESDAY

8:00	8:00	8:00
9:00	9:00	9:00
10:00	10:00	10:00
11:00	11:00	11:00
12:00	12:00	12:00
1:00	1:00	1:00
2:00	2:00	2:00
3:00	3:00	3:00
4:00	4:00	4:00
5:00	5:00	5:00
6:00	6:00	6:00
Evening	Evening	Evening
To Do	To Do	To Do

JANUARY						
S	M	T	W	T	F	S
						1
2	3	4	5	6	7	8
9	10	11	12	13	14	15
16	17	18	19	20	21	22
23	24	25	26	27	28	29
30	31					

2010

16 THURSDAY	17 FRIDAY	18 SATURDAY
Ashura		
8:00	8:00	
9:00	9:00	
10:00	10:00	
11:00	11:00	
12:00	12:00	**19 SUNDAY**
1:00	1:00	
2:00	2:00	
3:00	3:00	
4:00	4:00	
5:00	5:00	
6:00	6:00	NOTES
Evening	Evening	
To Do	To Do	

DECEMBER

DECEMBER
S M T W T F S
         1 2 3 4
5 6 7 8 9 10 11
12 13 14 15 16 17 18
19 20 21 22 23 24 25
26 27 28 29 30 31

20 MONDAY	21 TUESDAY ○	22 WEDNESDAY
	Total Lunar Eclipse	
	Winter Solstice / Yule begins	
8:00	8:00	8:00
9:00	9:00	9:00
10:00	10:00	10:00
11:00	11:00	11:00
12:00	12:00	12:00
1:00	1:00	1:00
2:00	2:00	2:00
3:00	3:00	3:00
4:00	4:00	4:00
5:00	5:00	5:00
6:00	6:00	6:00
Evening	Evening	Evening
To Do	To Do	To Do

JANUARY

S	M	T	W	T	F	S
						1
2	3	4	5	6	7	8
9	10	11	12	13	14	15
16	17	18	19	20	21	22
23	24	25	26	27	28	29
30	31					

2010

23 THURSDAY | 24 FRIDAY | 25 SATURDAY

Christmas Eve   *Christmas Day*

23 Thursday	24 Friday
8:00	8:00
9:00	9:00
10:00	10:00
11:00	11:00
12:00	12:00
1:00	1:00
2:00	2:00
3:00	3:00
4:00	4:00
5:00	5:00
6:00	6:00
Evening	Evening
To Do	To Do

26 SUNDAY

Boxing Day
Kwanzaa begins

NOTES

DECEMBER/JANUARY

DECEMBER

S	M	T	W	T	F	S
			1	2	3	4
5	6	7	8	9	10	11
12	13	14	15	16	17	18
19	20	21	22	23	24	25
26	27	28	29	30	31	

27 MONDAY ☾	28 TUESDAY	29 WEDNESDAY
8:00	8:00	8:00
9:00	9:00	9:00
10:00	10:00	10:00
11:00	11:00	11:00
12:00	12:00	12:00
1:00	1:00	1:00
2:00	2:00	2:00
3:00	3:00	3:00
4:00	4:00	4:00
5:00	5:00	5:00
6:00	6:00	6:00
Evening	Evening	Evening
To Do	To Do	To Do

JANUARY

S	M	T	W	T	F	S
						1
2	3	4	5	6	7	8
9	10	11	12	13	14	15
16	17	18	19	20	21	22
23	24	25	26	27	28	29
30	31					

2010/2011

30 THURSDAY	31 FRIDAY	1 SATURDAY
	New Year's Eve	*New Year's Day*
8:00	8:00	
9:00	9:00	
10:00	10:00	
11:00	11:00	
12:00	12:00	**2 SUNDAY**
1:00	1:00	
2:00	2:00	
3:00	3:00	
4:00	4:00	
5:00	5:00	
6:00	6:00	N O T E S
EVENING	EVENING	
To Do	To Do	

CONTRIBUTORS' NOTES

COVER

BARB SNYDER

The Gaze

8"x 10" gelatin silver print

For as long as I can remember I have always made things. It is an odd compulsion, this drive to assemble bits of things, to document ideas, record a colour, a texture or the feel of a thing. I only know that these aspects of sight and touch are deeply connected to emotions. Time and again, the process of 'making' has provided catharsis from deep, soul-searching grief or loneliness, as well as an outlet for joy and humour. Having no children of my own, my creations have formed part of my immediate family, surrounding me and keeping me company.

JANUARY

LINDA DAWN HAMMOND

Louise Lecavalier

8"x 10" gelatin silver negative

Linda Dawn Hammond works as a freelance photographer and journalist in Toronto, specializing in art, music, film and politics. As a fine art photographer, she has exhibited in North America and the UK. Her photography has been published in numerous books and periodicals, including *Cahiers du Cinéma*, *The London Times*, *Mojo* and *SXSWorld*. Hammond's photographic archives date back to 1976 and are primarily on the subjects of punk music culture and alternative film. They are presently undergoing a transition from analog to digital files, after which they will be made available on the internet as stock images.

Hammond earned a BFA in Photography at Concordia University, and an MFA at York University. A retrospective of her punk music photography, "Punks and Provocateurs," can be seen at rebelrebelle.com. Further information can be found at IndyFoto.com

FEBRUARY

JUDITH LERMER CRAWLEY

Creative Endeavours 1995

8"x 10" gelatin silver print

My work explores relationships, activities and interactions in social spaces and contexts. For me, the power of photography is linked to its ability to simultaneously refer to and interpret the visible world. This allows me to challenge stereotypes by looking at personal daily experience. Friends and family dominate my imagery.

Recent work explores my experience in connection with the effect of the Holocaust on my family's history. Other projects review the body of work I have amassed over more than 25 years. I am working on a website and continue to collect images of my community and travels. Work may be viewed at:

The Daybook Series — www.vaniercollege.qc.ca/audiovisual/slideshow/slideshow169/crawley/

About Auschwitz — www.vaniercollege.qc.ca/events/holocaust03/crawley_exhibition.html

Giving Birth is Just the Beginning: Women Speak about Mothering (photographs and text) is available for $25 (4551 Wilson Ave, Montreal, Quebec H4A 2V5).

MARCH

PAMELA HARRIS

The Clichettes

11" x 14" gelatin silver print

As a photographer I am given generous entry into a variety of lives, a happy fly on the wall in many worlds. I try less to imagine than to reflect, to be a window rather than a mirror. That is what delights me in photography.

> Major projects: the Canadian women's movement, an Arctic settlement, Mexican farmworkers, nannies, Newfoundland villages, my extended family.
>
> Permanent collections: California State Library, National Archives of Canada, McMaster University, City of Toronto Archives, York University, the Canadian Museum of Contemporary Photography and private collections.
>
> Books in print: *Faces of Feminism* (the project for which this photo was made) available from Sumach Press, and *Hot, Cold, Shy, Bold* (Kids Can Press). Out of print but still in libraries: *Another Way of Being*.

APRIL

VIRGINIA MAK

Anne Stevens

6" x 6" gelatin silver print

In this image, Anne enjoys a spontaneous moment of playfulness; I want to capture the essence of this moment. My recent work *Entranced* also depicts moments, quiet and frozen in time, where light and its passage through things creates abstract forms of subtle colours.

My work in photography touches on ideas such as the individual's relationship to culture and nature, internal dialogue, reflection and observation. Works I have exhibited include *Laundromat, Letter to My Mother, Side Street, Oh Ominous Sunshine, All I Work For, Summer* and *Hidden Nature.*

Born in Hong Kong, I studied philosophy at the University of Calgary and photography at the Ontario College of Art.

MAY

ELAINE BRIÈRE

Jeannie as Frida Kahlo

11" x 14" gelatin silver print

Elaine Brière is an award-winning filmmaker and photojournalist. *Testimony, Photographs of East Timor* was published in 2004 by Between the Lines. *Bitter Paradise: The Sell-out of East Timor,* won Best Political Documentary at the 1997 *Hot Docs!* film festival. Brière is currently in the Graduate Liberal Studies program at Simon Fraser University.

JUNE

EWA MONIKA ZEBROWSKI

Muse

8" x 10" gelatin silver print

Ewa Monika Zebrowski is a visual artist. who uses the camera to record her connections to places and people, to memory. Ms. Zebrowski's fine art and published experience spans ten years. Her images can be found in private and public collections in Canada, the

United States and Italy. She has had ten solo exhibitionas and participated in numerous group shows. Ewa Zebrowski is represented by the gallery Art Mûr in Montreal, where she lives with her husband and two sons.

Ewa Zebrowski's photographs resemble moving images, for they are less concerned with an arrested moment than with the mystery of time steeping towards a moment. One feels the light changing even as one looks; intensifying, reaching greatest potency, whether toward darkness or radiance. This imbues each image with a profound poignancy, for each photograph is a small story of desire, of a life beyond grasp, lost to us or never found, or at the aching brim of becoming. Desire is a kind of grief, and Ewa Zebrowski's photographs are replete with this desire.

— *Anne Michaels*

JULY

LYNN MURRAY

Sonda Turner Nampijinpa
Environmental portrait, digital print

I have been a photographer since 1971. When I was 25, I became fascinated by the social changes happening in Chile. With the help of a Canada Council grant I arrived just in time to document the final four months of Salvador Allende's socialist government, and kept a diary. I had to leave with the help of the Canadian Embassy; I remember the newspaper headlines as I left: "25,000 Foreigners, 25,000 Terrorists, Denounce Them!" When I returned I exhibited the photographs, and then put them away. In September 2008, after they had sat in my closet for 35 years, I was persuaded to show them at Gallery 44, along with my diary. This has given me renewed energy to continue my photography; I am now working with the Solidaridad Museum Group on collecting the history of Latin American immigrants in Canada.

AUGUST

LAURA WATT

Trish with Textile Work
8"x 10" gelatin silver print

Laura Watt is a lifelong resident of east end Toronto, where she lives with her film-making husband, orange cat and white dog. Coming from a long line of creative women, Laura is currently expecting her first child and is interested in finding out what the next generation will create.

As a graduate of the Ontario College of Art and Design, she earned her AOCAD in Fine Arts Printmaking in 2002. Laura has shown her work extensively, both locally and abroad. Currently her artistic focus has been on a series of watercolour paintings, yet she finds herself easily distracted in favour of another creative act, vegetable gardening.

SEPTEMBER

LOUISE ABBOTT

Mary Cartmel Sculpting a Murder of Crows
8"x 10" gelatin silver print

As a long-time writer, photographer and film-maker in the Eastern Townships of Quebec, I have concentrated on documenting rural life and the natural environment in Canada and abroad. My latest book is *The Heart of the Farm* (Montreal: Price-Patterson, 2008), produced in collaboration with my husband, photographer Niels Jensen. Through our small business, Rural Route Communications, Niels and I have also produced two companion video documentaries: *Crisscrossing Space and Time* and *Giving Shelter*. In 2008 we helped to establish an artists' cooperative and art gallery called Studio Georgeville. We are currently at work on a book and video documentary about the Cree of James Bay.

OCTOBER

JILL GLESSING

Women's Words — Barbara Gowdy
8" x 10" gelatin silver print

Jill Glessing lives, teaches, writes and photographs in Toronto. She has worked in photojournalism, experimental imagery, still life and portraiture. A range of her work has been exhibited and published. She currently teaches art and academic studies at the Ontario College of Art and Design and York University.

NOVEMBER

MARY LOUISE CHOWN

Art on the Job
Digital Image

I am a storyteller, visual artist, and musician. I love the old mythologies and folktales, and the ways in which they can still speak to us. I like to think that all the elements of life can be found in the creative arts — the commonplace transformed into the extraordinary through our imagination. I love the ease with which the digital camera can capture an image that at first glance may seem so ordinary, yet on further examination reveals a complex situation. It's another way to tell stories to all ages.

DECEMBER

SHEILAGH ETHNE O'LEARY

Anne
11" x 14" gelatin silver print

Sheilagh Ethne O'Leary is an established award-winning art photographer born and living in St. John's, Newfoundland. Her work has been exhibited and collected internationally and appears in numerous art journals and publications. Sheilagh received her art education through mentorship with Manfred Buchheit, Concordia University's Faculty of Fine Art, Banff Centre for the Arts and the Rockport Maine Workshops.

Her passion for people drives her to produce striking collections of nudes and portraits with an intimate exploration of the subject and their relationship to the Newfoundland landscape. Her most recent project published by Boulder Publications is an art book titled *Human Natured: Newfoundland Nudes*, which explores almost two decades of her black-and-white nude photography.
www.sheilagholeary.com

ABC

ADDRESSES / TELEPHONE NUMBERS

DEF

GHI

OPQ

RS

TUV

MENSTRUAL/HEALTH CALENDAR

	1	2	3	4	5	6	7	8	9	10	11	12	13	14	15	16	17	18	19	20	21	22	23	24	25	26	27	28	29	30	31
JAN																															
FEB																															
MAR																															
APR																															
MAY																															
JUNE																															
JULY																															
AUG																															
SEPT																															
OCT																															
NOV																															
DEC																															

Ovulation occurs 12-14 days before the first day of your period; you will have about 5 days of stretchy, sperm-friendly mucous before ovulation. This is your fertile period in the cycle.

YEARLY PLANNER 2010

JANUARY

Sunday	Monday	Tuesday	Wednesday	Thursday	Friday	Saturday
					1	2
3	4	5	6	7	8	9
10	11	12	13	14	15	16
17	18	19	20	21	22	23
24 / 31	25	26	27	28	29	30

FEBRUARY

Sunday	Monday	Tuesday	Wednesday	Thursday	Friday	Saturday
	1	2	3	4	5	6
7	8	9	10	11	12	13
14	15	16	17	18	19	20
21 / 28	22	23	24	25	26	27

MARCH

Sunday	Monday	Tuesday	Wednesday	Thursday	Friday	Saturday
	1	2	3	4	5	6
7	8	9	10	11	12	13
14	15	16	17	18	19	20
21	22	23	24	25	26	27
28	29	30	31			

YEARLY PLANNER 2010

APRIL

SUNDAY	MONDAY	TUESDAY	WEDNESDAY	THURSDAY	FRIDAY	SATURDAY
				1	2	3
4	5	6	7	8	9	10
11	12	13	14	15	16	17
18	19	20	21	22	23	24
25	26	27	28	29	30	

MAY

SUNDAY	MONDAY	TUESDAY	WEDNESDAY	THURSDAY	FRIDAY	SATURDAY
						1
2	3	4	5	6	7	8
9	10	11	12	13	14	15
16	17	18	19	20	21	22
23 / 30	24 / 31	25	26	27	28	29

JUNE

SUNDAY	MONDAY	TUESDAY	WEDNESDAY	THURSDAY	FRIDAY	SATURDAY
		1	2	3	4	5
6	7	8	9	10	11	12
13	14	15	16	17	18	19
20	21	22	23	24	25	26
27	28	29	30			

YEARLY PLANNER 2010

JULY

Sunday	Monday	Tuesday	Wednesday	Thursday	Friday	Saturday
				1	2	3
4	5	6	7	8	9	10
11	12	13	14	15	16	17
18	19	20	21	22	23	24
25	26	27	28	29	30	31

AUGUST

Sunday	Monday	Tuesday	Wednesday	Thursday	Friday	Saturday
1	2	3	4	5	6	7
8	9	10	11	12	13	14
15	16	17	18	19	20	21
22	23	24	25	26	27	28
29	30	31				

SEPTEMBER

Sunday	Monday	Tuesday	Wednesday	Thursday	Friday	Saturday
			1	2	3	4
5	6	7	8	9	10	11
12	13	14	15	16	17	18
19	20	21	22	23	24	25
26	27	28	29	30		

YEARLY PLANNER 2010

OCTOBER

Sunday	Monday	Tuesday	Wednesday	Thursday	Friday	Saturday
					1	2
3	4	5	6	7	8	9
10	11	12	13	14	15	16
17	18	19	20	21	22	23
24 / 31	25	26	27	28	29	30

NOVEMBER

Sunday	Monday	Tuesday	Wednesday	Thursday	Friday	Saturday
	1	2	3	4	5	6
7	8	9	10	11	12	13
14	15	16	17	18	19	20
21	22	23	24	25	26	27
28	29	30				

DECEMBER

Sunday	Monday	Tuesday	Wednesday	Thursday	Friday	Saturday
			1	2	3	4
5	6	7	8	9	10	11
12	13	14	15	16	17	18
19	20	21	22	23	24	25
26	27	28	29	30	31	

▽ 2010 ▽

JANUARY
S M T W T F S

                        1 2
3 4 5 6 7 8 9
10 11 12 13 14 15 16
17 18 19 20 21 22 23
24 25 26 27 28 29 30
31

FEBRUARY
S M T W T F S

   1 2 3 4 5 6
7 8 9 10 11 12 13
14 15 16 17 18 19 20
21 22 23 24 25 26 27
28

MARCH
S M T W T F S

   1 2 3 4 5 6
7 8 9 10 11 12 13
14 15 16 17 18 19 20
21 22 23 24 25 26 27
28 29 30 31

APRIL
S M T W T F S

              1 2 3
4 5 6 7 8 9 10
11 12 13 14 15 16 17
18 19 20 21 22 23 24
25 26 27 28 29 30

MAY
S M T W T F S

                        1
2 3 4 5 6 7 8
9 10 11 12 13 14 15
16 17 18 19 20 21 22
23 24 25 26 27 28 29
30 31

JUNE
S M T W T F S

        1 2 3 4 5
6 7 8 9 10 11 12
13 14 15 16 17 18 19
20 21 22 23 24 25 26
27 28 29 30

JULY
S M T W T F S

              1 2 3
4 5 6 7 8 9 10
11 12 13 14 15 16 17
18 19 20 21 22 23 24
25 26 27 28 29 30 31

AUGUST
S M T W T F S

1 2 3 4 5 6 7
8 9 10 11 12 13 14
15 16 17 18 19 20 21
22 23 24 25 26 27 28
29 30 31

SEPTEMBER
S M T W T F S

            1 2 3 4
5 6 7 8 9 10 11
12 13 14 15 16 17 18
19 20 21 22 23 24 25
26 27 28 29 30

OCTOBER
S M T W T F S

                      1 2
3 4 5 6 7 8 9
10 11 12 13 14 15 16
17 18 19 20 21 22 23
24 25 26 27 28 29 30
31

NOVEMBER
S M T W T F S

   1 2 3 4 5 6
7 8 9 10 11 12 13
14 15 16 17 18 19 20
21 22 23 24 25 26 27
28 29 30

DECEMBER
S M T W T F S

            1 2 3 4
5 6 7 8 9 10 11
12 13 14 15 16 17 18
19 20 21 22 23 24 25
26 27 28 29 30 31

2011

JANUARY
S M T W T F S

                  1
2 3 4 5 6 7 8
9 10 11 12 13 14 15
16 17 18 19 20 21 22
23 24 25 26 27 28 29
30 31

FEBRUARY
S M T W T F S

       1 2 3 4 5
6 7 8 9 10 11 12
13 14 15 16 17 18 19
20 21 22 23 24 25 26
27 28

MARCH
S M T W T F S

       1 2 3 4 5
6 7 8 9 10 11 12
13 14 15 16 17 18 19
20 21 22 23 24 25 26
27 28 29 30 31

APRIL
S M T W T F S

              1 2
3 4 5 6 7 8 9
10 11 12 13 14 15 16
17 18 19 20 21 22 23
24 25 26 27 28 29 30

MAY
S M T W T F S

1 2 3 4 5 6 7
8 9 10 11 12 13 14
15 16 17 18 19 20 21
22 23 24 25 26 27 28
29 30 31

JUNE
S M T W T F S

          1 2 3 4
5 6 7 8 9 10 11
12 13 14 15 16 17 18
19 20 21 22 23 24 25
26 27 28 29 30

JULY
S M T W T F S

              1 2
3 4 5 6 7 8 9
10 11 12 13 14 15 16
17 18 19 20 21 22 23
24 25 26 27 28 29 30
31

AUGUST
S M T W T F S

  1 2 3 4 5 6
7 8 9 10 11 12 13
14 15 16 17 18 19 20
21 22 23 24 25 26 27
28 29 30 31

SEPTEMBER
S M T W T F S

            1 2 3
4 5 6 7 8 9 10
11 12 13 14 15 16 17
18 19 20 21 22 23 24
25 26 27 28 29 30

OCTOBER
S M T W T F S

                  1
2 3 4 5 6 7 8
9 10 11 12 13 14 15
16 17 18 19 20 21 22
23 24 25 26 27 28 29
30 31

NOVEMBER
S M T W T F S

      1 2 3 4 5
6 7 8 9 10 11 12
13 14 15 16 17 18 19
20 21 22 23 24 25 26
27 28 29 30

DECEMBER
S M T W T F S

            1 2 3
4 5 6 7 8 9 10
11 12 13 14 15 16 17
18 19 20 21 22 23 24
25 26 27 28 29 30 31

NOTES

IMPORTANT TELEPHONE NUMBERS

DOCTOR

PHARMACY

DENTIST

POLICE

DAYCARE

SCHOOL

BABYSITTER

BANK

LAWYER

IN CASE OF EMERGENCY   Name   Telephone
Address

NEW & INTERESTING FROM SUMACH PRESS

FICTION...

IN A PALE BLUE LIGHT *Lily Poritz Miller*
THE EXCLUSION PRINCIPLE *Leona Gom*
THE SHERPA AND OTHER FICTIONS *Nila Gupta*
ARGUING WITH THE STORM *Rhea Tregebov (ed)*
THE BOOK OF MARY *Gail Sidonie Sobat*

SUMACH MYSTERIES...

RAGGED CHAIN *Vivian Meyer*
ILLEGALLY DEAD *Joan Donaldson-Yarmey*
ON PAIN OF DEATH *Jan Rehner*
BOTTOM BRACKET *Vivian Meyer*

FOR YOUNG ADULTS...

GWEN *Carolyn Pogue*
CLEAVAGE: BREAKAWAY FICTION FOR REAL GIRLS
Deb Loughead and Jocelyn Shipley (eds)
HEALER'S TOUCH *Anne Gray*
WATCHING JULY *Christine Hart*
SWAHILI FOR BEGINNERS *Lisa Joyal*
WINGS OF A BEE by *Julie Roorda*
RITES OF THE HEALER *Anne Gray*
FEAST OF LIGHTS *Ellen S. Jaffe*
MELLA AND THE N'ANGA: AN AFRICAN TALE *Gail Nyoka*
SERAPHINA'S CIRCLE *Jocelyn Shipley*
TIME AND AGAIN *Deb Loughead*

NON-FICTION...

WHO'S YOUR DADDY? AND OTHER WRITINGS ON QUEER PARENTING *Rachel Epstein (ed.)*
WHOSE UNIVERSITY IS IT ANYWAY? POWER & PRIVILEGE ON GENDERED TERRAIN *Anne Wagner et al.*
BRANDING MISS G__: THIRD WAVE FEMINISTS AND THE MEDIA *Michelle Miller*
D IS FOR DARING: THE WOMEN BEHIND THE FILMS OF STUDIO D *Gail Vanstone*
A CHANGE OF PLANS: WOMEN'S DTORIES OF HEMORRHAGIC STROKE *Sharon Dale Stone*
TRANS/FORMING FEMINISMS: TRANSFEMINIST VOICES SPEAK OUT *Krista Scott-Dixon (ed)*
WILD FIRE: ART AS ACTIVISM *Deborah Barndt (ed)*

Check our website for other exciting reading —
www.sumachpress.com